Online Reputation:

Your Most Valuable Asset
in a Digital Age

By Sarah Pearce

Edited by Kaitlyn Shiels

HOUSE OF WORDS PUBLISHING

What others are saying about this book:

"You could risk spending a small fortune on reputation damage control or you could simply read this book. A comprehensive look at the do's and don'ts when it comes to the age of digital reputation with scary case studies to ensure you are kept on your toes. This is a must read for any business or individual who uses social media and the Internet as a tool, and will become a go-to manual for all to abide by. Sarah Pearce puts all the tech stuff that we so need to be aware of into logical language that makes sense. Whether you are a social media beginner or think you are a pro – there is huge take-home value in this timely read."

—JIMMY MURRAY,
CEO, PROPERTY NOISE GROUP (NZ)

"A thoroughly fascinating and frightening look at how the way we do business has changed with the evolution of the Internet and how a good online reputation is crucial! A must-read for everyone from individuals, to marketing personnel to business owners. It is imperative to understand that what we put online will always be there and can affect anything from a job application to a lawsuit. The interspersed real-life stories are enough to make you sit up and think twice about all your online interactions. If I had written a book on ethical online presence and social media – this would have been it!"

—LEILA SUMMERS,
AUTHOR AND MARKETING COACH

"We all know that today, because of the convergence technologies, good news travels fast and bad news travels even faster! In the old days if you upset someone through bad customer service you'd be lucky if they only told 10 people about their experience. Today they can rant about you and your brand to millions before they've even left your car park. Make no mistake, right or wrong, the Internet has become word of mouth on steroids. With this in mind, smart people will educate themselves with tips, tactics and strategies on how to combat and protect your greatest asset online – your reputation. Your education starts with this book and I recommend you read it today to protect yourself and your brand from becoming "Digital Dust". You've been warned!"

—SCOTT WILSON,
HEAD OF SALES & MARKETING, DIGITAL INFLUENCE

"Reputation management is something that has not always been a key focus in New Zealand. But living in a country where we are all only 2 degrees away from each other, it is vital. Sarah Pearce manages to really dig deep on the important points and uses some amazing stories to illustrate the importance. Social media is here and it is not going away, so get smart and read this book!"

—STEPHEN MARTIN,
HEAD OF VIRTUALSTAFF NZ.

"Many businesses worry about their online reputation – and with good reason, because a careless tweet, candid Instagram photo, or humorous Facebook post can destroy a reputation that took years to build. But most businesses don't know how to protect, preserve, and enhance their reputation. Sarah Pearce has the answer! This book is a practical, up-to-date and insightful guide for all business owners and leaders. It's packed with wise ideas and instructive case studies, and is a 'must-have' reference for anybody who cares about their online reputation."

—GIHAN PERERA,
FUTURIST AND SPEAKER, GIHANPERERA.COM

"The premise is pretty straight forward: Whether you're a brand, an individual or a "brandividual", online reputation is an increasingly influential contributor to your success. Or failure. What Sarah Pearce sets out to do in this book is provide all the relevant information any person or company needs and help them to build, manage, monitor and protect their online reputation. What you find on the search and social Web becomes a very important first or second impression. As a business professional responsible for being in the public eye or managing business communications and marketing, being able to assess and affect how people see you online should be a top priority. The good news is that Sarah provides a handy framework for taking control over how you and your brand are known online and shows you how to build a trusted online presence with a foundation too strong for a reputation wrecking ball to penetrate. It is a great and "must do" read for anyone involved in the digital world - and these days that is just about everyone."

—PHILLIP QUAY,
CEO, MEDIAPA

Online Reputation:
Your Most Valuable Asset in a Digital Age
By Sarah Pearce

© 2015 House of Words Publishing

ISBN 978-0-473-34154-1 (Softcover – mono interior)
ISBN 978-0-473-34476-4 (Softcover – colour interior)
ISBN 978-0-473-34156-5 (Kindle)
ISBN 978-0-473-34155-8 (ePDF)

Editor: Kaitlyn Shiels
Design/Typesetting: Chris Moore – www.fromprinttoebook.com

sarahpearce.co.nz

Disclaimer:

The information contained in this book is of a general nature and should not be relied upon in lieu of specific information and advice from service and legal professionals which would be tailored to meet your personal and business situation.

This book is not intended as a substitute for legal or Search Engine Reputation Management advice. The specific facts that apply to your matter may make the outcome different than would be anticipated by you.

Neither the author nor the publisher shall be held liable or responsible to any person or entity with respect to any loss or incidental or consequential damages caused, or alleged to have been caused, directly or indirectly, by the information or examples contained herein. All information, statistics and websites mentioned were correct at the time of publishing.

Thankyou.

This book is dedicated to my sons,
Theo and Carlos,
who first taught me about computers fifteen years ago.

And to my amazing partner, Ian.

Acknowledgements

A special thanks to the following:

Kaitlyn Shiels, for her talent and hard work.

Chris Moore, for his kindness and creativity.

Troy Rawhiti-Forbes, who took time out of his busy schedule
to write the foreword.

Gina Korczak, for telling me this book should be
an online course – and then making it happen.

And Ian Wafer, who made it all possible.

Contents

Foreword 8

Introduction 10

A Global Village 13

Your Message to the World 17

Five Minutes to Ruin 21

The Way We Were 27

Digital Footprints and Digital Shadows 39

Everything Leaves a Trail 43

The Ostrich Effect 47

The 7 Deadly Sins of Online Behaviour 49

If You Want to Hide a Dead Body… 57

How to Outshine the Competition 71

The Corporate Shift to See-Through 75

Biggest Transparency Failures 77

Reputation Bombs 81

Stop the Bleeding 87

Understanding Branding 95

Build a Brand with These Tools 103

Keeping Your Finger on the Pulse 111

Unleash the Power of LinkedIn 115

Rules of Engagement 119

Attract and Engage 125

Your Guide to the Top 133

Avoid Extinction 145

Bibliography 148

About the Author 155

Foreword

Troy Rawhiti-Forbes

I'm going to date myself terribly by writing this, but it's one of those timeless lessons that we all need to be reminded of sometimes.
You may have watched a movie or read a book where one character, upon meeting the hero, says something like "your reputation precedes you." That happens in real life too, and in my case the Internet had a lot to do with it.

I applied for a job in 2007, some ten years after I first got my feet wet in social media. The job was a newsroom role at the New Zealand Herald's website and the editor, an enthusiastic and kind fellow named Jeremy Rees, cut me off before I could begin to describe myself. Why? Because I didn't have to. I'd already done it. You see, Jeremy had read my MySpace profile, and so he had already formed an impression of me. The interview, it turned out, was to find out whether I had the same kind of personality in the flesh as I was online; whether or not we could work on the same team. Was I good value as someone to go to war with or share a drink with?

My reputation had preceded me. Past Me had done Contemporary Me a huge favour by being a decent human being, and the job was mine.

There are two values I try to maintain when I'm conducting any online activity – whether it's for my day job at a very big and reputable corporate, or when I'm talking junk about video games or sharing pictures of remarkable things I see on my way to work. The first is simply this: Don't be a dick. Don't gasp, gentle soul, because there are worse words on the Internet, and if you've got any front-facing roles then you or your front-liners are going to hear them.

You protect your reputation by behaving in a reputable fashion.
It's pretty simple, right? That means meeting kindness with kindness,
hostility with patience, and everything with respect.

The second value is a personal one to me, but you can skin it
in your own way: Don't disappoint mum. My mum only follows me
on Facebook, but if I feel like I'm sailing close to the wind anywhere,
I ask myself if she'd be disappointed to pick up what I'm putting down.
What I'm really talking about here though is to consider your
stakeholders and your community, internally and externally.
The community's reputation is yours, and vice versa.

The great thing, and also the challenging thing, is that nothing is set
in stone. The Internet's built on shifting sands, and so is your reputation
online. It's up to you to continue watching, nurturing, growing, and
correcting whenever you need to.

I'll leave you here, and Sarah's going to take over. You'll read a number
of fascinating case studies, some happened years ago. Why will you be
reading them here? For starters, they're relevant to your interests and
they're integral to your professional development. You're here to learn.
Lesson one is this: Once it's online, it's there forever.

It may even end up in a book.

Troy Rawhiti-Forbes.
Social Strategist and Communities Manager,
Spark NZ, @TroyRF, Auckland, New Zealand
October 2015

Introduction

Unless you have been living in a bubble over the past 10 years, you realise how dependent the world has become on social media. The days of hand writing a letter, addressing an envelope, and sending it to the desired recipient are becoming obsolete. No longer do you have to wait for days for a response via snail mail. Now you simply log on to your social media account, just a few clicks and you are on your way to reaching whomever it is you need to speak with.

Tweets, reviews, and online comments have become some of the most impactful indicators of a brand's success in the eyes of consumers. Potential customers are now turning to Yelp and Facebook pages when deciding where to take their business. But when not all feedback is positive, how do we defend ourselves against unpleasant reviews and online attacks? More importantly, how do we re-establish our value to potential customers?

While social media has countless positive benefits, it is also capable of putting both businesses and individuals in real danger of ruined reputations. All it takes is that one unfavorable post, tasteless selfie, or ruthless rebuttal. Often times, people react without thinking in everyday situations. It is no different when dealing with social media. However, because of the instant access, speed and reach in this space, the repercussions can be deadly to your reputation – and globally seen.

Online Reputation: Your Most Valuable Asset In A Digital Age, provides you with the tools you need to effectively manage your online image.

- You will learn the do's and don'ts of social media: How many tweets per day is too much? What is deemed acceptable to post on Facebook? And what kind of content should you be uploading to YouTube?

- You will be provided with case studies of ruined online reputations so that you may learn from the mistakes of others.

- And I will show you how to build a trusted online presence with a foundation too strong for a reputation wrecking ball to penetrate.

In an online world in which real selves are invisible, every move we make is amplified. It all sends a powerful message about us to the rest of the world. Don't allow yourself to fall prey to a catastrophic character collapse caused by even the most minor indiscretions. Before you reach for that selfie stick, pick up this book and learn how to shine in cyberspace.

A Global Village

With the advent of the Internet, our world has changed forever. We now live in an age of great transparency and connectedness. Privacy, as we know it, is a thing of the past. The way we search for things, the way we form and conduct relationships, and the way in which we trust will never be the same. We have become a global village.

As a result of the instant access, speed, and reach of online and social media, everyone now has a voice. This outlet and its ability to be heard has created a level playing field and completely shifted the balance of power between consumer and company.

Choosing to be unaware of this change and the impact it has on us makes us vulnerable – vulnerable to being left behind and vulnerable to no longer being relevant to the consumer. If we allow this, we are creating a gap that our competitors will fill by providing a superior – and more relevant – customer experience.

More than 3 billion people around the world (that's closing in on half the global population) now use the Internet (Kemp, 2015). What's more, 2 billion people have social media accounts (Kemp, 2015). Of these social media users, 70% are online every single day (Valant, 2013).

With this surge of connectedness, it is no surprise then that the way in which we purchase has changed also. It is reported that 89% of the Internet population now research a product, business or service online first before they purchase (Griwert, 2012).

As a business professional, your engagement online builds trust, creates brand awareness, and cultivates valuable relationships. Many people are suspicious or overwhelmed by the fast-paced world of social media, but it is very much like socialising in real life: you talk, listen, and then respond. It is the digital form of word of mouth.

Primarily, this book serves as a guide for the business community on navigating the online world. Its intention is to impress upon readers the importance of building a good online reputation, and its feasibility and measurability in terms of success in this borderless digital world.

Almost by default, we have all inherited a virtual identity. Alike to the "real world," everything we do and say in this online reality also sends a message and is an act of communication to the rest of the world.

We are always communicating, even when we may not be aware of it. When conducting business, most of us take heed to control and manage the visual part of this communication – our presentation – at least, to some degree.

When we deliberately and consciously manage this message of presentation, we are 'positioning the product' as it is known in the marketing world. In small business especially, we must carefully position ourselves first in order to approach the customer or client, before selling our product.

Conducting business in this digital marketplace is similar to the offline world. Successfully positioning ourselves for the market is important. Creating social media accounts and setting up a review forum for your business may not be too difficult, but navigating the online world and presenting that all-important message correctly is a bit tricky.

This book will walk you through the steps of creating and maintaining that ever-important message online by way of reputation management, brand identity, and tips on how to do it better than your competition. The main focus is to create an awareness of the social media pitfalls so they can be avoided. Additionally, it shows you how a powerful and positive digital presence will, not only work as a buffer against negative feedback, but it will help grow your business and brand, while connecting you with existing and potential clients and peers.

As members of the business community, we must constantly be aware of the shifts in technology that alter the professional world. To turn a blind-eye is a sure way to be left behind, and in a market in which relevance is key, this mistake is destructive to business.

Your Message to the World

Your brand name is only as good
as your reputation.

–RICHARD BRANSON

Your reputation is a message that others 'read' about you before they meet you. Like a social resume, it goes out before you and will either open up new opportunities, or it will slam them shut. A good business is built on excellent service and a great reputation.

The building blocks of this foundation are trust, relationships, and communication. Social media has made a visible shift in the way in which these blocks are formed. It emphasizes the impact the online world has on our personal lives, careers, and businesses.

How do we create and relay this message? Offline, we position ourselves through factors such as our office location, the type of car we drive, the style of clothing we wear, the places we choose to dine, the brands we associate with, and countless other choices that create our image. Even the tiniest of details is important. In the offline world, the factors that contribute to the way we are seen by others are multifaceted; we usually can and do control them.

Online, we are constantly communicating. Even if we try not to be seen and opt out of having a digital presence, we are still sending a message. Excuse the double negative, but we cannot not communicate, and in the digital age, the message sent from our online persona is even more powerful.

First and foremost, our online presence has global reach. We are no longer bound by geographical limitations, but rather are conducting business in a global marketplace. Secondly, in the online world where our real selves aren't visible, everything we do and say is magnified.

In the absence of physical world cues and information that we can see and pick up on, our online presence cultivates the opinion that others form of us. This lack of face-to-face insight is how the online image can become quite skewed from 'reality.'

Although the digital world may seem like a separate reality, it absolutely impacts our 'real world' business. It affects potential clients' perceptions of us when they are deciding if we are credible, professional, likeable, and trustworthy. It especially impacts the final decision of customers when they are weighing whether to work with us or our competition.

What does that mean to you as a business owner or professional?
It means that while you are busy dressing up nice, polishing your
shoes, cleaning your car, signing off on your print promotions,
putting flowers on your desk, and getting ready to meet your
consumers in the 'real world,' most of them have already met
you first…online. This begs the question: how do you look online?

First impressions are powerful and lasting. When we say
"first impression," we are referring to a deeply ingrained mental
bias that forms almost instantly upon meeting a person. This rings
true both in person and online. According to researchers at the
Missouri University of Science and Technology, it takes two-tenths
of a second for an online observer to form an impression about you
(Belicove, 2012).

As Digital Analyst and Futurist, Brian Solis says, "Customer
experience happens with or without direct interaction with marketing.
If I use a product, look at your website or come across your campaign,
these things happen without the company knowing my impressions,
my expressions or what I say about them to others" *(Brian Solis
direct email newsletter, 21 Sep, 2015).*

For example, if someone skimming over your online actions finds
you tedious, offensive, or even just guilty of being a bit sloppy in
punctuation, this will influence how he or she sees you as a person.
Even if this person meets you face to face later on and decides you
were wrongly judged, that initial perception is still going to be hard
to shake.

Making a great first impression, both online and offline, should be
one of your business priorities. Living in a super-connected, always-on,
and constantly changing digital world may have changed many things
for all of us, but the value of a first impression, along with the power
of a good reputation, remains constant.

Five Minutes to Ruin

It takes a long time to build a good reputation. Brick by brick, stone by stone, you watch as it grows strong. Then one stupid mistake can come in like a wrecking ball and destroy all your hard work in an instant.

–Pam Martin

Reputation can be defined as the general perception or belief that others have formed about you, your brand, and your business. It is a form of social proof, and a collective view of you. Your reputation is an expectation set forth indicating that you will behave a certain way and ensures that you can be trusted to behave this way fairly consistently. A reputation helps you gain or lose trust before you even meet someone.

Have you thought long and hard about your company's reputation? Can you remember when you made a conscious effort to enhance this reputation? Review sites are more popular than ever now, so chances are you have been forced to consider your company's reputation through the comments of others. Take some time to consider the following questions: What is your hiring process like? How would others view your company's culture? How dedicated are you in satisfying both your employees and your customers? Why is this all so important?

In business, a good reputation is gold. Businesses with great reputations endure longer and recover quicker when hard times hit all. They are perceived as providing more value and find it much easier to recruit while having less issues with retention.

As a business professional, your reputation is everything. It tells others you are worth working with and that you can be trusted. This helps you stand out from the crowd and receive maximum value for your work.

In his article in *Psychology Today*, Dr. Lickerman (2009) said, "A good reputation represents a great marketing strategy. When I find a service provider of any kind whose performance outshines their competition, they become like gold to me. I use them repeatedly, recommend them enthusiastically to others, and don't begrudge paying them what they're worth."

Reputation is often confused with brand and character. In simple terms, your brand is how you *want* others to think about you. Your reputation is what others actually *do* think about you, and your character is *who* you really are. Throughout this book, you will find case studies alike to the following. These "Reputation Wrecking Balls" narrate individuals and brands that have learned the destructive potential of online actions the hard way so that you don't have to.

 REPUTATION WRECKING BALL

Intimidation Gone Wrong

Once a fairly regarded place to stay, the Union Street Guest House in upstate New York showcased pleasant decor, a boutique-like atmosphere, and tasty food. The hotel realised the importance of improving its online reputation by encouraging positive reviews versus negatives reviews. Makes sense, right? Well, how they went about it ruined the hotel's reputation. This company threatened its members with financial penalties if they posted anything unfavorable.

Although the hotel believed it was preventing slander,
it instead did the exact opposite. People viewed the company
as a corporate villain, which caused the hotel to alienate itself
from potential guests.

How could a company fine a customer for posting an
uncomplimentary review? Unfortunately, this is not a fictional
tale. The hotel's policy stated, "If you have booked the Inn for
a wedding or other type of event anywhere in the region and
given us a deposit of any kind for guests to stay at USGH there
will be a $500 fine that will be deducted from your deposit for
every negative review of USGH placed on any Internet site by
anyone in your party and/or attending your wedding or event.
If you stay here to attend a wedding anywhere in the area and
leave us a negative review on any Internet site you agree to
a $500 fine for each negative review" (DeMers, 2014).

Several reviewers retaliated and protested against this policy
by posting numerous negative comments about the hotel.
Of course, these reviews included the unfair policy the
company put in place, along with many other of the hotel's
flaws. This led to a one-and-a-half star rating on Yelp, and press
releases highlighting the intimidation. Consequently, business
declined, and the hotel, along with many other businesses
learned a valuable lesson that scare tactics NEVER work
(DeMers, 2014).

"It takes 20 years to build a reputation and five minutes to ruin it,"
Warren Buffet said. These days, reputations, many that have been
years in the making, are being ruined in an instant online. This is
largely due to online users being unaware of the incredible power and
reach of the Internet and uneducated on how to manage and control
their digital footprints. Many companies do not have sound online

risk management policies in place and typically only take action when threats arise. This is not reputation management; it is crisis management and a reactive rather than proactive approach.

For the most part, the online world is referred to as an entirely separate entity to the 'real world.' What most people don't seem to quite understand is the real life implications that can come as a result of something being said online. We are all aware of those individuals and brands who continue to be visible in the media, but for all the wrong reasons. Even large global brands are vulnerable to finding themselves with a damaged online reputation. With all of the intricacies to follow and adapt to in the online world, it's no wonder that companies so often slip up. Here is another example.

REPUTATION WRECKING BALL

DiGiorno's Tweet in Bad Taste

Frequently, brands see trending hashtags and take it as an opportunity to jump on the bandwagon and receive instant exposure. Generally speaking, this is a good tactic to use, but it's crucial to be fully aware of what the hashtag refers to and ensure that it in no way has the potential to implicate the brand. DiGiorno Pizza made a massive blunder in 2014 when they jumped on the #WhyIStayed hashtag. The hashtag campaign was meant to bring to light the hidden issue of domestic violence and lend a voice to victims. Unfortunately, the account manager for DiGiorno didn't seem to clue in and tweeted, "#WhyIStayed You had pizza" (Short, 2014).

Immediately, DiGiorno was the target of (somewhat deserved) backlash. Countless individuals began tweeting at them about how much they were personally victimized and offended by the tweet. In under a minute, the pizza company had deleted the tweet, but it astoundingly had already drawn the attention of most of the globe on social media. Moments later, the account tweeted an apology, explaining that it had misinterpreted what the hashtag was about as it hadn't clicked through to see the other tweets. Subsequently, the DiGiorno account spent hours going through and ensuring that it directly apologised to each person who had responded to their offensive tweet.

What you post online has the potential to reach millions and last forever so ensure that you know the ins and outs of online reputation management before diving in.

The Way We Were

*The digital world is no longer 'the way
of the future' – that was 5 years ago –
it is NOW.*

–Annah Stretton

In an ever-changing world, it makes sense that the way we buy,
sell, search, and connect has also drastically changed and evolves
continuously. With smartphones, hotspots, and portable devices in
everyone's hands, online is where both the traffic and the people are.
If you aren't online, you are invisible. If you aren't visible, connected
and looking good online, you will get outsold by your competitors
who are making their strengths known.

To fully understand how to protect ourselves and our business in
a constantly changing world, let's look briefly at how the fundamental
shift in trust, privacy and communication have all impacted on us
in this digital age.

Ways of Communication

Prior to the Internet, our primary means of communication was
in person, in writing and by telephone. Today, the way in which
we communicate on a daily basis has been completely revolutionised,
and the majority of society has not only accepted, but embraced this
change. Meeting face to face with a person or talking with him or her
by phone is becoming less and less common. Smartphones, emails
and social media are now the most popular ways of connecting.

There are some critics that feel all of our online connecting is
making us increasingly unsociable. On the other end of the spectrum,
others are quick to point out the Internet is simply another *way*

of communicating and it allows us to connect and build relationships more so than before. In days past, we would socialize and communicate with our circle – family, friends, and our local community. Now, with the globalisation we have in this digital age, we have few limits on who we can connect with. Social media has enabled many to reconnect and stay in touch with family, friends, and acquaintances with whom they had previously lost contact. Effectively, we have become globally sociable on a scale where we once were only locally sociable.

Given the customer service world is so people-based, it is vital that business professionals understand and adjust to these changes in order to future-proof their business. They need to fully grasp that their current and future customers continue to shift from physical interaction to virtual interaction.

Having a business that continues to be based solely around traditional methods of communication is now too restrictive. Yes, it is vital to be knowledgeable, credible, hardworking, skilled and professional to be successful – that's a given, but business success is also heavily reliant on relationships – old and new. Excellent communication, networking, being seen and being top of mind is key. People deal with those they know, like, and trust…and trust is the prized currency of social media.

Savvy professionals treat socialising online as they do socialising offline. Strategically, they use it to get involved with their community

and connect with their local market on a personal level. Social media allows you to put character and personality into your brand that would not otherwise be possible without having face to face conversations. It makes a static "About" page on a business website come to life. Activity on social platforms plays out this information in real-time, colourful action, rather than simply "telling."

All About the People

For salespeople especially, people will often choose your competition over you because they have already spent months, and even years, building a relationship with them.

Social media provides a valuable opportunity to build this relationship with your specific target market too. You will meet and connect with people you may never have met before offline. As well as initiating and developing new connections, social media allows you to remain in touch with your clients. This ensures that you are top of mind to call when they are ready to make another business transaction.

New tech based engagement has changed us both personally and professionally. Ultimately, we now have access to more people at greater distances and with increased speed.

Breaking News in Real Time

Social media hasn't only changed the size of our networks, it has also accelerated the speed of our communication. A message that used to take days and sometimes weeks to be sent, can now be sent and received within a matter of seconds.

These days, when disaster strikes, the world hears about it as it is happening. Breaking news rolls out in real time via videos, live streams, status updates, and shared images. We no longer have to reach for a newspaper, or tune in to the six o'clock news. By simply picking up our smartphones, the world news lies in the palm of our hands.

It goes without saying that this speed in communication has deeply impacted the society we live in. What's more is its impact on the way we do business and how it has affected the interaction among consumers, brands and companies.

Previously, product or service dissatisfaction would be expressed by way of a typed or handwritten letter sent to the manager of a company. This act was undertaken by the consumer in the hope – but with no great confidence – that the message would be read at the other end.

What a sense of achievement, if not the feeling of a small miracle, if a response was made and a satisfactory outcome achieved. Back in those days, all the power was in the company's hands. To the consumer's benefit, this is no longer the case.

Social media has created a level playing field and completely shifted the balance of power between consumer and company. It has given everyone a voice. Consumers are now able to voice their dissatisfaction direct to company and the company is forced to listen, or at the very least be *seen* to be listening – because the issue is now in a public arena with a highly engaged audience. The company's reputation (and therefore future profitability) is now at stake. The following is an example of a company forced to learn a harsh and expensive lesson about *not* listening.

United Airlines Breaks Guitars

In 2009, transportation titan, United Airlines, found itself
the target of a viral hate-campaign. A musician by the name
of David Carroll was set to travel by way of United to Nebraska
with a layover in Chicago. At the end of the first half of his trip,
Carroll noticed that the baggage crew of the airline were carelessly
handling passengers belongings, including his guitars. Concerned
for the state of his beloved instruments, he asked for help from
the airline and requested the crew take better care in handling
the baggage. When there was no course of action taken,
Carroll complained, but was still unheard. Upon arriving at
his destination, the musician discovered that one of his guitars
– which was worth $2,500 – had been damaged beyond repair.

Furious, David Carroll sought compensation from United Airlines
but was ultimately refused. A resourceful and creative individual,
Carroll chose to share his experience the best way he knew how.
He created a music video and posted it on his YouTube channel.
The video was titled "United Airlines Breaks Guitars."

The video garnered 8 million views in 8 months. Carroll did
a total of 300 media interviews and he made Time Magazine's
list of Top 10 Viral Videos of the year. As a result of this
incident, United Airlines lost $180 million dollars in dropped
share value, and learnt a very expensive lesson. The airway
did eventually apologize, but it was much too late to save their
reputation. It is said that United uses "United Breaks Guitars"
in their employee training videos, emphasizing the power of
customer opinion (davecarrollmusic.com).

Customer Expectations

Thanks to Google and social media, consumers have come to expect instant gratification in customer service, especially when it comes to communication. As Solis (2011) points out, consumers no longer see decent customer service as an optional extra, but as their right. Should they not get it, they vote with their feet and take their business elsewhere, but not before they voice their reasons loud and clear on social media as they go.

Those out-dated businesses that still only offer a toll free number for customer service are in grave danger of extinction. Why would one choose to be a client of a company that keeps their clients waiting on the line for long periods of their time? Even more irritating, once the call is finally answered, to encounter customer service staff who are mostly disempowered to truly resolve the issue.

In contrast, those businesses that continue to move with the times, listen to their consumers, and care about the experience they provide them, are also usually those that realise the importance of a strong social media presence. They have a well-trained team employed to handle consumer feedback via their social platforms and they *engage* directly with their audience. Their Facebook page welcomes consumers to write comments directly on their wall. They publically respond to tweets. In this way, they not only manage and protect their reputation, but through being "real", transparent, and caring, they earn trust and brand collateral.

This sort of "now" communication is what turns detractors into fans, customers into followers and followers into brand advocates. These customers voluntarily and enthusiastically spread the word about that business to the market, thereby helping them to grow in the most powerful way: organically.

Tons of Fancy Gadgets

In just the last 25 years, the cyberspace environment, with its many sophisticated social platforms, has also transformed the ways we connect. Remember snail mail, telegraph, and faxes? These ways of communicating now seem practically prehistoric.

Today, everyone has tons of fancy gadgets – smartphones, tablets and laptops most common. We tend to organise our lives, in particular our social lives, through some form of technology. Facebook reported back in 2011 that 57% of us talk more online than face to face (Hepburn, 2011). That is more than half of us!

In business, the more ways you communicate yourself and your product to your target market, the greater your chances of success. Integrating online advertising and social media marketing with traditional methods will help you reach new clients that traditional marketing methods alone would never have reached. Use those new modes of communication to your business and brand advantage.

Transparency

Previously, it took considerable time, effort and research to find out about a person or a business. We would have to do some scouring – encyclopedias, press releases, articles dug up in journals – and even then we ran the risk of still not being able to find what we were looking for. Now, we have Google at our every beck and call.

It seems that, in our age of limited privacy, few things can be hidden or buried. This unlimited access to information has forced businesses to be held more accountable. Consequently, companies are increasingly adopting business transparency as their policy. There is more on this subject in a later chapter.

Permanence

Prior to the Internet, we humans had the mixed blessing of being able to forget. "Time heals" was a popular mantra. Today, we have a new mantra: "The Internet remembers everything!" Forgotten your friend's birthday? No problem: Facebook will remind you.

The subject of how to handle a relationship breakup in an online world has now become the subject of many advice columnists and is further evidence of this change in permanence. The key problem being a difficulty to 'forgive and forget' when the 'Ex' keeps making appearances on social media, often clearly happy and having 'moved on' to the next person.

What about all the shared memories and relationship milestones that were once lovingly noted online? Once something goes on the Internet, it is nearly impossible to completely remove it.

Consumers may throw out last week's newspaper with that editorial expressing a frustrating customer experience, but Google will be sure to pull up the online version in its search results. Social media certainly has changed the way we experience life.

Trust

As discussed, we now live in an age of transparency and connectedness. This means that privacy as we knew it has all but gone, and the way we trust has been transformed.

In her 2010 TED talk, Rachel Botsman, guru of the Sharing Economy, said, "All this new technology is enabling trust between strangers. We used to be wary of people we didn't know. We taught our children not to talk to strangers. Today, we not only talk to strangers, but we share our lives with them and call them our friends" (Botsman, 2010).

What's more, according to a 2013 study, over 88% of us now *trust* online product reviews from strangers (often anonymous) and we trust them almost as much as we trust personal recommendations from our friends and family (Anderson, 2014).

We have also become accustomed to sharing our licenses, passports, credit card details and other sensitive information online, so long as the website boasts a little padlock icon.

This next story of reputation ruin was caused by a child sharing a private family situation with her facebook friends…and beyond.

Reputation Wrecking Ball

Expensive Facebook Post

Who has one of those family stories in which a child blurts out something he or she shouldn't have? Generally, the child unknowing says something rude or offensive amongst family members or out in public to which the parent is immediately embarrassed and profusely apologizes. Such stories are often told as a humorous, fond memory. Here, we look at a case that isn't quite as humorous when a daughter's "blurt" online cost her parents $80,000.

Upon winning that sum as a settlement in a discrimination complaint with his ex-employer, the daughter of the claimant took to Facebook to express her joy. The girl posted: "Mama and Papa Snay won the case against Gulliver. Gulliver is now officially paying for my holiday to Europe this summer. SUCK IT" (Stucker, 2014). Of the daughter's 1,200 Facebook followers, many were students of Gulliver school (Stucker, 2014). As anyone could guess, word quickly spread and it was just days later that the father received a letter from the school's attorneys, informing the family that they would not be receiving the $80,000 settlement as the daughter broke their confidentiality agreement (Stucker, 2014). Despite appeals, the court leaned in favor of the school and the daughter's single Facebook post cost her parents $80,000, and her, a trip to Europe.

Sometimes we must look back before we look forward. After assessing the way in which the world has changed since the dawn of the Internet, we are better equipped to protect our online reputation. Awareness is the first step. The next step is to understand that how we are seen in the digital space is made up partly by our actions – and partly by the online actions of others.

Digital Footprints and Digital Shadows

In the future your digital footprint will carry far more weight than anything you might include on a resume.

–Chris Betcher

Our world has gone online and taken us with it. We all now have a virtual self and, along with it, a virtual reputation. What does this mean to you? Everything you do and say online sends a powerful message about you to the rest of the world. This message shapes your digital persona and impacts your digital reputation. What we do online and the content we contribute is referred to as our digital footprint.

What's the catch? Well, this message about you is also determined by others. The actions of others in regards to you (and your reaction to them) all affects how your virtual persona is perceived. The term 'shadows' is used to refer to content posted by others that contribute to your online identity. What *others* post that reflects on us is called our digital shadow. Together, our digital footprints and our digital shadows complete our identity and impact our reputation.

In the 2011 Google Public Policy blog post, Tuerk said, "your online identity is determined not only by what you post, but also by what others post about you – whether a mention in a blog post, a photo tag or a reply to a public status update" (Tuerk, 2011).

Unfortunately, those who contribute to our online messages are not always people we are friendly with. These digital shadows can often come from an old relationship, former friends, disgruntled employees, competitors, or others who may have a vested interest in making you look bad. Sometimes the shadows on your reputation can be generated by those who acted with the best of intentions, as you will see in this next case study…

 Reputation Wrecking Ball

The Star Wars Selfie

In one such case, it was not what the victim posted that ruined his reputation, but the careless assumptions of another.

A man was out at a local shopping center when he came across a Star Wars display. He thought that his children, who are avid Star Wars fans, would love to see it. Hence, he did what many may have done and took a 'selfie.' A woman nearby was out shopping with her children, saw this man take the photo, and immediately assumed that he was taking photos of her children. Because the man had also spoken to the children earlier, the woman jumped to the conclusion that the man was a predator and reported him to police. Rather than just reporting and leaving it to officials, the woman used social media to bring the man down. She had taken a photo of him in the store, shared the image, and wrote an angry post accusing him of being a "creep" and preying on children.

The image went viral on social media and soon reached the man's family. His wife first saw the image of her husband with warnings labelling him as a child predator and was immediately horrified. He went to the police to clear up the confusion and set the record straight but his reputation was already damaged (Leonard, 2015).

The constant access and viral spread capabilities of social media can turn false accusations and moments of ill judgement into repercussions that can destroy lives.

To ensure that you are always on your best behaviour and are always practicing proper social media etiquette, think: would I want the employer of my dream job to see this? What about my grandmother? Your (future) children? If the answer is no, it is best to simply hit that little 'x' button. Whether it be about ourselves, a family member, an institution, or a complete stranger, the effects of negligent online behaviour can be devastating to a reputation.

Even the content posted by your family and friends will affect the way you are perceived online. Consider the photos you're tagged in while at social events, Christmas parties, and celebrations – are they showing you the way you would like to be perceived by the entire world – professionally or personally? These days it's not just about who you know; it is also about who knows you!

Everything Leaves a Trail

Goodbye mystery; hello Social Media
(aka Oversharers Not-So-Anonymous).

–Ali Polin

In present times, people expect a good business or trusted practitioner to have some digital presence. It is the new normal. To have no online presence raises a question – even subliminally. At the very least, it doesn't send a message of a business who is confident with new technology or determined to be relevant to consumers who are now increasingly present in the digital space.

Yet, to some degree, having an abandoned social media profile can look worse than having no online presence at all. A poorly set up, abandoned, or incomplete social media account indicates lack of follow-through and commitment. Potential clients will see it and wonder, "If they can't even keep on top of their digital presence, how well will they be able to handle what I need?"

The same principle applies in the way your website represents you. It is your storefront and the digital face of your brand. That being said, what impression do others get about you when it holds outdated information, spelling mistakes, dangling client enquires or is simply cumbersome to operate and not optimized for mobile device viewing? Clients are likely to assume that you are inconsistent and unprofessional. Rather, you want your websites to showcase that you pay great attention to detail, demonstrate professionalism, and are confident with new technology.

One of the worst offences in abandoning online presence is poor communication with online reviews and questions asked on business pages. When a business does not respond to queries and comments from past, current, or potential clients in a timely manner, they are made to feel unimportant and neglected. As a result, they view the offending business as unreliable.

Obviously, being visible is important, but what else affects your online impression? How about the communities you belong to, the groups you support, the questionable jokes you may have liked and the public forums you have ranted on? Everything paints a picture. Everything leaves a trail.

It's difficult to navigate the online realm and to always ensure that you're putting your best foot forward when it comes to your business. There are new social norms to follow, always a new social platform emerging, and it's difficult to communicate your message clearly without that vital face-to-face connection. I am sure that all of us have been guilty, at one point or another, of finishing a particularly rough day at work and venting about it to a partner, friend, or family member. It helps to get your frustrations off your chest and it's reassuring to have someone lend an ear and support you. While it's only natural (and generally harmless) to vent to someone close to you, problems arise when that frustrated individual turns to social media to blow off steam.

Whenever you make a post, you run the risk of broadcasting that content to the world. Through liking, commenting, reposting, retweeting, and sharing, others in our circles can pass along that content, exposing it to an entirely new audience. From there, someone in that circle can share it and so on and so forth. This next case study shows somebody losing their job before they had even fully won it – all thanks to one careless tweet.

When Tweets Costs Jobs

There have been multiple cases in which employees, or would-be employees, posted something controversial on social media, leading them to be fired. In 2009, NBC News reporter, Helen Popkin, reported a case in which an almost-hired candidate of Cisco IT company, lost her would-be job in just 140 characters. Upon being offered the position she had recently interviewed for, the careless individual tweeted: "Cisco just offered me a job! Now I have to weigh up the utility of a fatty paycheck against the daily commute to San Jose and hating the work" (Popkin, 2009). I'm sure the woman thought nothing of it when she hit "tweet," thinking her followers may find it humorous and she might get a few favorites.

Unfortunately for the woman behind the account, her reckless tweet was seen by a Cisco employee. The employee responded by saying "Who is the hiring manager. I'm sure they would love to know that you will hate the work. We here at Cisco are versed in the Web." Almost immediately, the would-be employee's account was set to private and all incriminating tweets were deleted. However, as is the case with anything on the Internet, you can't simply delete and move on.

The errors made by the woman went viral and Internet supersleuths revealed her "real life" identity. This lady's mistake sparked Internet memes to be made about her and a website with the deleted content was created to immortalize her poor judgement. In posting a simple, thoughtless tweet, she not only ruined her chance of being hired for the position, but destroyed her online reputation.

Almost everything you do online can be seen and traced. Permanently deleting a message once it's out there is almost impossible. It doesn't matter what kind of device you are using or how you are searching and behaving online, it can all be traced back to the source. Think of the online communities you belong to, the groups you support, the content you "like", and the forums you post in, this all paints a picture that forms your online identity.

The Ostrich Effect

Some try to opt out of social media altogether. "Oh, but I don't do social media," they say, "I just don't get involved." Those who choose this path think that they are saving themselves time and effort and reducing the danger of getting it all wrong. This is what I call "The Ostrich Effect." The truth is, burying your head in the sand will not protect you. Rather, for businesses, it does much more harm than good. You can try to have nothing to do with social media, but in reality, it's just going to happen without you. The only difference is you may not be aware of it.

As Eric Qualman of *Socialnomics* says: "We don't have a choice in
if we do social media, we only have a choice in how well we do it"
(Cruz, 2011). Yes, you will save time updating your statuses and
posting new content, but you will really be doing yourself a disservice.
While you may not *appear* online, your lack of presence will reflect to
most as being out of touch and disconnected. It certainly won't keep
you top of mind to prospective clients.

The best route to take is to be consistently aware, engaged, and
influencing the conversation. As Zarrella, author of *Social Media
Marketing* says, "Users are already talking about your products,
services and brand online, whether you are involved in the discussion
or not – so you may as well join the conversation" (Zarrella, 2009)

Our world is now a seamless integration of online and offline
platforms. The Internet has changed everything.

Brian Solis wrote about this in his 2011 book, *The End of Business
As Usual*: "Every so often, the events that emerge and play out before
us are so transformative that evolution is disrupted, giving way to
a revolution. The effects affect social development, human behavior
and ultimately the course of history" (Solis, 2011).

He added that, "We need to explore avenues to shape and steer
experiences rather than discount how technology is changing
behavior" (Solis, 2011). The opportunity for **reach**, **impact**, and
influence, and their effect to create the potential for thousands of
new clients for your business is too big to be missed. The trick now
is to learn the right way (and avoid the very wrong way) to do this.

The 7 Deadly Sins of Online Behaviour

Greed, envy, sloth, pride and gluttony:
these are not vices anymore. No, these are
marketing tools. Lust is our way of life.
Envy is just a nudge toward another sale...

–JON FOREMAN

Some of these 7 Deadly Sins of Online Behaviour may appear obvious or as common sense, so why do many people commit these social media sins daily, resulting in severe reputation damage? While the goal of social media is to be visible and extend your reach, it is important to ensure that you aren't making common mistakes that will have you visible online in all the wrong ways.

Sin 1. Posting when emotional (or drunk)

This is yet another instance of how an error in judgement made online, can impact us quite differently – and often more severely – than that same mistake would affect us offline. It's human nature to get swept up in the heat of the moment, get a little bit carried away, and to say or act in a manner you typically wouldn't. Whether it was due to being overly emotional or at the hands of alcohol, we usually regret it, feel shameful or embarrassed, and move on within a few days. As with many instances though, when this happens

online, it has a much more lasting impact and can ruin your entire reputation.

Not posting when emotional or intoxicated may seem obvious, but you'd be surprised to see how many people have made this mistake. With inhibitions lowered, the transgressor takes to social media to overshare. It might have been an incriminating or embarrassing photo, or perhaps an inappropriate tweet, but by the time the people behind the posts have collected themselves, it's all too likely that their indiscretions have been viewed by many.

Photos can be saved, screenshots can be captured, and shares and retweets can go viral. Google will always cache (store) pages, and a popular website called the Wayback Machine has saved every single webpage since 1996. All content you create, will be captured and archived forever, making it impossible to delete and forget.

There are countless websites dedicated to the cringe-worthy content people post online – check out Lamebook.com for some good ones – that have been captured by social network "friends." It's imperative to only post when you're at your best and always triple-check the appropriateness of what you're sharing.

Sin 2. Telling lies

In the digital age with the world at our fingertips, fact checking is quick and easy. One of the most detrimental things you can do to your reputation is make false statements. Eventually, and usually rather quickly, the truth comes to light and all brand equity will be lost.

In 2013, the Deputy Editor of CNN-IBN and a well-respected media figure, Sagarika Ghose, was apparently dissatisfied by speeches given by Gujaret's Chief Minister Narendra Modi at a news conference. Rather than keeping her opinions to herself, she turned to social media in an effort to perpetuate the dissatisfaction with Modi. On her Twitter account, Ghose claimed that the Chief Minister didn't stay to take questions from the press. With as much exposure as media personnel have, the tweet spread like wildfire. Her tweet was confirmed by other media representatives to be false and her professional credibility took a hit (Matsuo, 2014).

Through just one deceiving post, that painstakingly, valuable trust earned over time can be shattered in seconds.

Sin 3. Posting negative comments about a client

Posting negative comments about your boss is almost always detrimental, but airing a client's dirty laundry can be equally, or even more damaging. One of the main goals in online marketing is to create a long-lasting relationship with your customers based on trust and loyalty; posting something negative about them online (or anywhere) destroys those virtues. Who wants to do business with someone who is snarky and makes rude comments behind your back? Reflect before you remark!

Sin 4. Posting inappropriate or compromising photos

A picture says a thousand words and you always want to consider what yours is saying. Posting an inappropriate photo – even if it might only be considered inappropriate to just *some* of your audience – is a bad idea. Several social media websites are heavily visual;

as a result, we hear countless horror stories of those who've shared a compromising image and received backlash.

In maintaining your online reputation, it's exceptionally important to carefully monitor the photos you are "tagged" in. Almost everyone has a smartphone with a camera and most people use them frequently. Always play it safe and make yourself aware of photos being taken before they end up on social media. Does this mean you should stay out of photos while having fun with family, friends and colleagues? Certainly not. However, be aware of what's being captured and be mindful to monitor whether or not it lands online.

If a person does happen to catch you off-guard in a compromising photo, quickly "untag" the image so that it no longer appears on your profile or in your photos. If you let the person who posted politely know that you'd rather not have that photo seen by the world, chances are he or she will remove it. Incidentally, Facebook has over 170 privacy settings…How many of them do you know or use? (McKeon, 2010). I imagine the person in this next story would have a very different view of social media after making an epic error in judgment that quickly became visible all over the globe.

REPUTATION WRECKING BALL

Halloween Horror-Story

We've all made clothing mistakes, right? Most of us can think back to a costume choice that makes us cringe. In 2013, a naive 22-year-old female from Michigan, U.S., dressed up in a running skirt, t-shirt, and road-race bib. She added faux gashes, fake blood, and bruises to her face and body, all to attend her office Halloween party. Assuming she was being humorous, this young woman called her costume a "Boston Marathon Bombing Victim," then posted photos of herself in it on her social media accounts (Giacobbe, 2014).

The posts went viral and the public backlash was instant. The woman became the target of a modern-day witch hunt. She received death threats and rape threats. Harassers started showing up at her home and her workplace to confront her. When her boss heard of the story, he was swift to fire her before she further risked the company's reputation.

For weeks, this woman was bombarded with nasty comments, death threats, and constant harassment. An error in judgment and a foolish social media post claimed another victim. Before the age of social media, the woman would not have received nearly as much attention. She may have been gossiped about at the office and sent home to change her outfit, but in the age of social media, her immature mistake was exposed to the whole world including the victims of marathon bombings (Giacobbe, 2014). It is important to take care to consider how your actions and posts may be perceived by others. Something humorous and light to you may be deeply offensive to another. It is always best to keep your online presence free of comment on social or political issues, and anything that may be offensive to other people.

Sin 5. Reacting defensively

Defensive behaviour is rarely appreciated; this is true in the online world too. If you receive criticism or backlash for anything you've posted or shared, the worst thing you could do is lose your cool and get defensive.

When individuals get their backs up, they come off as heated and aggressive. This does not solve an issue. What can you do to keep your composure? Take a breath, pull yourself together, and imagine yourself in the other person's shoes. What is it that may have been offensive or inappropriate to them? Can you understand why they may have felt this way? Always take the high road and calmly diffuse the situation.

Sin 6. Refusing to apologise

Apologising is rarely easy for most and doing so online is no exception. While it may be difficult to combat stubbornness and say you're sorry, it's much more difficult to perform damage control from the aftermath that usually comes after refusing to apologise. Standing your ground is not worth risking your online reputation. Publically make amends, and then move on. Learn from the situation and improve your service as a result. By doing so, you will gain the respect of others.

As humans, we all make mistakes. It's how we handle the aftermath of these mistakes that defines our character. Think about this the next time apologising might be difficult to do. You'll thank yourself in the long run.

Sin 7. Ignoring complaints

The deadliest online sin, far worse than refusing to apologise, is ignoring complaints entirely. Whether it be that you're unsure of how to properly respond, or that you feel you shouldn't dignify it with a response, the truth remains that ignoring a complaint won't make it go away. If you don't listen the complainants will just shout louder, and then they will create a facebook page dedicated to their cause and invite the rest of the world to join.

Facing complaints head on is the best practice in dealing with them. Customers appreciate a person who takes ownership for his or her actions. In facing the issue, you assure others on the other end that you genuinely care about what they have to say and wish to work to resolve it. Some of the most successful brands are not those that strive for or claim perfection, but those that address issues head-on, work to make things right, and appreciate customer feedback. Shying away from complaints is never the right course of action and will only bring more dissatisfaction. Furthermore, as Lee Resource states – be they vocal or silent, "91% of dissatisfied customers will not do business with you again" (Digby, 2010).

You are wise to be mindful of these deadly sins and avoid them at all costs. Poor behavior is poor behavior and the consequences of this are only magnified online. Think of social media as a conversation. Let your customers talk. Listen to them and use the feedback to learn how to treat them better. In the long run, it will pay off for your business. Always remember, social media is not a quick fix, it is part of a long term strategy to customer growth.

If You Want to Hide a Dead Body…

–Todd Jensen

While everything happens faster in the digital age, developing an ethical online reputation doesn't. It takes time and dedication to cultivate an image that will build trust and connect you with current and potential customers. As is the way outside of the digital world, first impressions are everything and building a good reputation takes commitment.

Most people don't look past the first page of Google search. We look up something online and only read the first page of search results. This tendency has become such a widespread phenomenon that jokes and memes have been made about it: "If you want to hide a dead body put it on the second page of Google" (Georgia Local Marketing, 2014).

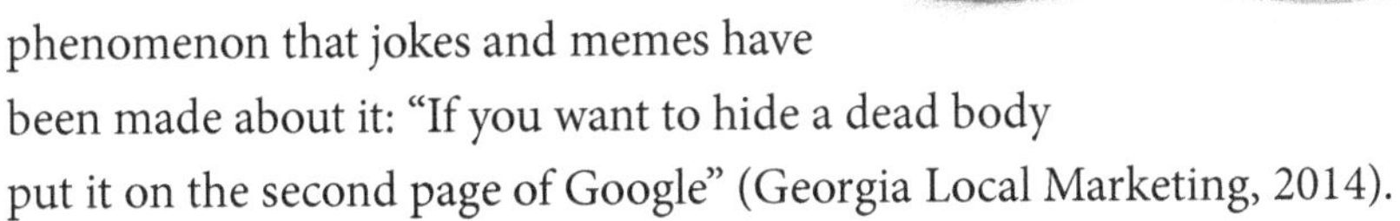

With this in mind, think of Google's first page as your business card. You want to own it. When anyone searches you or your business, you want to show up on the front page looking great.

By following these steps, you will jumpstart your way to creating an effective and reputable online presence and brand.

Step 1. Claim Your Brand Online

Take control of what is written about you. Though you may not be able to directly stop people from posting negative things about you, you can ensure you know what is being said and keep track of what is posted through several websites such as KnowEm.com. This website helps individuals and businesses alike keep track of anything that is posted about them on social media. Through detailed web-scraping, KnowEm sweeps the Internet for personal names, business titles, or any other keyword you may be searching for. This website is an invaluable tool that helps individuals and businesses discover and secure their name across social media. In addition, KnowEm shows users how to "contact each site in order to have their name released and returned to them" (KnowEm.com).

There are several websites alike to KnowEm that will scour the Internet to pick up on posts made about you. Socialmention.com is another such site that can be used by individuals and businesses to track their name and find out what is being posted. Social Mention scans over 100 social media platforms to be sure that no post created is missed.

Another option to consider is Reputation.com. This is a company that strives to create a good reputation for individuals and businesses. In an interview with O'Hara, the founder of Reputation.com, Michael Fertik, spoke about managing online reputations. Here, he discussed the importance of creating a Google Alert for yourself, using Twitter a few times per month rather than tweeting every day, posting fewer photos on social media, and avoiding using Facebook frequently without a thorough understanding of the privacy settings. Fertik added that "if you don't know who the joker is on your social media page, it's you" (O'Hara, 2013). Not only will Reputation.com identify the negative posts, but it will work with you to push those posts down in search rank, ensuring that they won't be the first to pop up in search results.

Knowledge is power and by identifying the negative attention you've been given online, you can take steps to counter them and decrease their value. Always be one step ahead to ensure you are never caught off guard by negativity.

Step 2. Set Up Alerts for News About Yourself/Brand

As previously mentioned in summarizing Michael Fertik's social media tips, you can create email notifications for the things you search for through Google Alerts. Rather than obsessively using a search engine to check for mention of your name or brand, let Google Alerts take over as it continuously reaches out into the world of the Web with your alerts in mind.

Setting up Google Alerts is simple. If you already have a Google account, be sure that you're logged in. The beauty in having a Google account is that you can access hundreds of services from one username: Google Docs, Gmail, YouTube, etc. Once logged in, simply input the keywords or triggers that you'd like to track. For starters, you should create an alert for your name, business name, and your website. From there, simply change the settings for your alerts to suit you. You can mark what type of content you'd like to receive, how often you want to get emails, and the volume of search results you want to see.

It would be smart to consider creating an alert for each of your employees, your spouse, or any other persons who are directly (and even indirectly) related to your business. Who you associate yourself and your business with will ultimately reflect on you. Therefore, be careful not to let the reputation of another affect yours. This may seem like an extreme measure, but we live

in a world in which it is widely considered common practice to search
a potential hire before we even meet the person!

Step 3. Secure Domain Names and Social Media Handles

Purchasing a domain name, regardless of whether or not you intend
to launch a website, is highly recommended by many experts in the
industry. In her article for Forbes, legal and business columnist
Susan Adams, shared what she learned first-hand from the leaders
of reputation management websites. In addition to Googling yourself
and setting alerts, one insistent piece of advice was to buy your own
domain name.

Some experts, like CEO and Co-Founder of Brand Yourself,
Patrick Ambron, said to snatch as many domain names as possible
related to your business. If you're set on a name and have considered
the lasting power of it, purchase the corresponding domains in
several variations. For example, you have set up a new real-estate
business, Preferred Properties, and want to make sure it has a
strong online presence. You are thrilled to discover that www.
preferredproperties.com is still available. However, in taking
Ambron's advice, you would not only purchase this domain but
purchase the .org, .net, .me, alternatives. Taking this one step further,
you could pre-emptively avoid potential customer mistakes and
purchase www.preferredproperty.com and later have them all redirect
to your main site. In doing this, you are ensuring that no one else can
choose to purchase your domain before you do. For businesses that
heavily rely on e-commerce and leads generated from the Web,
this option is one to seriously consider.

For most, however, creating one domain will suffice. When it comes
to personal websites, portfolios, and those unassociated with a business
name, it is widely considered "Better to pick one domain name and

put some effort into creating content that will live on the site."
For content, consider what will highlight your skills and sell yourself
to those viewing your website. "You can write a short bio of yourself,
a story from your life, and include your CV. This is also a place to
post interesting articles and your own commentary about them"
(Adams, 2013).

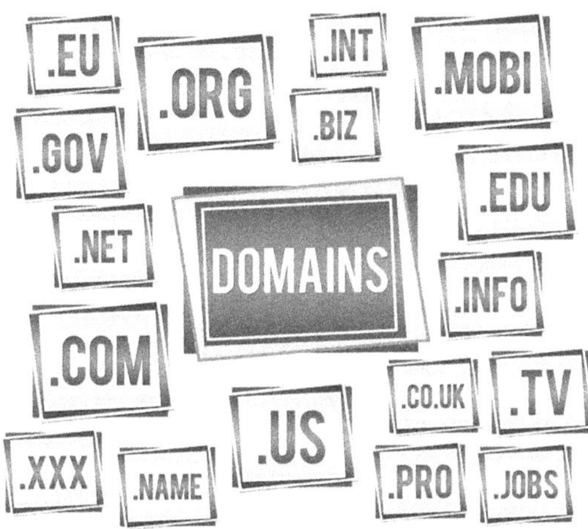

Once you've secured your domain name by purchasing it from a web-hosting site such as Go Daddy or Bluehost, spend some time securing corresponding usernames on various social media platforms. If a happy customer of Preferred Properties wanted to tweet a positive review to the business's Twitter account, it would prove difficult for that customer to find the page if it were under a different username. Avoid this confusion by registering usernames on Facebook, Instagram, Twitter, YouTube, and other major social networking platforms. The consistency in the promotion of your brand is key in appearing professional and composed.

Before purchasing a domain, it is a good idea to do a little research and ensure that your desired usernames are available. Namechk.com is an invaluable tool that will check the availability of your desired username.

Step 4. Google Yourself

One of the first places someone turns to when wanting to learn information about another person is Google. Employers Google potential hires, patients turn to Google when selecting a doctor, and some of us have even been guilty of Googling the names of our dates. Turn the tables around and Google yourself! It is important to see what information can be discovered about you. Most commonly, the first results are social media profiles. With this information in hand, consider your privacy settings as anyone with a smartphone or access to the Internet can see your personal profiles just by searching your name. While it may be true that most people won't look past the first or second pages of Google, it doesn't hurt to dig a little deeper and ensure that nothing negative or incriminating would pop up for the thorough searcher.

Now that you've seen the search results on the first few pages, take it one step further. A picture is worth a thousand words, which is exactly why it's important to perform an image search. Are the photos that are coming up professional headshots from your LinkedIn profile? Or, are they a candid holiday shot that a friend had posted and tagged you in? When your online reputation is a top priority, you value and take pride in what you allow others to see.

Pete Kistler, Co-Founder of Brand Yourself, shared a personal experience that led him to founding the company. In 2008, Pete was looking for an internship, but wasn't having much luck finding one. He searched his name on Google, only to discover that there is a convicted drug dealer who shared his exact name. Potential employers had been performing a simple Google search, and concluded that the Pete Kistler whose resume they were considering, was a convicted felon. This experience led Kistler to team up with Patrick Ambron, the current CEO of BrandYourself, to create positive online content and help other push down other negative content (Adams, 2013).

Step 5. Build Your "Virtual Real Estate"

Once you've purchased your domain name and secured your social media accounts, it's important to add quality content to your pages. It would be futile to secure a business meeting with an important potential client, only to arrive at the meeting with nothing to say or to show!

The industry you are in will dictate what you choose to share across your platforms. For many, creating an online portfolio or collection of works that best represent what you offer is the way to go. Ask past clients if they wouldn't mind you adding the work you did for them to your portfolio. If you need to "bulk it up" and have minimal past projects, research what type of work potential clients are looking for and create an example of something similar. Once your portfolio is created, add it to your networks. LinkedIn is a great resource for displaying your projects. You might consider creating one on Portfoliobox.net or ViewBook.com, and simply referencing the link. Regularly updating your portfolio is imperative. Your online presence requires frequent maintenance, because you want to ensure that what the world sees is a true reflection of your current skills.

One of the most vital aspects in creating a strong online presence is building your reputation on social media. While you don't *need* to spend hours each day maintaining every possible social network, it is a good idea to pick three accounts that will really work for your business and focus on them. Going back to Preferred Properties, the owner might choose to focus on Instagram, Facebook, and YouTube. With a business relying so heavily on visual elements, choosing the networks that focus heavily on photography will really highlight what they have to offer. Social networks are also outstanding ways for companies to interact with their customers and respond to feedback.

Maintaining a presence on social media is crucial for business. Here's why: According to a 2014 study conducted by Pew Research Center, 74% of all Internet users belong to and use a social media website. That large percentage of people is an audience of potential customers that you have the opportunity to impress and interact with each and every day.

Many consumers consult social media before making a purchasing decision. It's common to check a restaurant's Facebook page for its menu before dining, or to look up a boutique's Instagram for a sample product before deciding to visit. A lack of social media presence will often make potential customers turn to another business that offers what yours doesn't.

Simply having a page won't attract a loyal following. It takes regular maintenance to keep your networks up to date and engaging.

While this does take time, consider a few options to help you manage. You can hire a Social Media Manager or add the task to the job description for the employee in charge of your marketing. If you'd rather be in control of your accounts, consider signing up for HooteSuite.com. Designed for social media management, HootSuite allows you to create and pre-schedule posts. This will enable you to create and schedule a week of posts at one time rather than having to create new content each day.

Regardless of the platforms your prefer, or the methods of maintenance that you choose, one thing rings true: social media is one of your best resources for business outreach. Ensure that you are searchable, engaging, attentive, and that your message is compelling.

Step 6. Humanise Your Brand

Today, it seems as though anyone and everyone has a blog. Why? Well, blogging proves to be beneficial. Forbes recently published an article titled "The Top 10 Benefits of Blogging on Your Website." In this article, columnist Jayson DeMers, discusses the ways in which businesses can positively grow from hosting a regularly updated blog. In order to reap the most benefits, he mentions that hosting your blog on your business site is the smartest move. DeMers writes that "While hosting a blog independent of your business site is better than not having one at all, you'll see that many of the benefits below can only be achieved if your blog is hosted on your primary domain (i.e.,www.your_site.com/blog)" (DeMers, 2015).

What are these benefits DeMers mentions? The first is that the additional content increases your ranking in search engines. Search Engine Optimization (SEO) is quite complicated and it would take an entirely separate book to explain it clearly. Essentially, the more pages your website has the more times your site is indexed in search engines. DeMers explains this with a fishing analogy. He writes that the "more hooks you have in the water, the more likely you are to catch a fish" (DeMers, 2015). With every blog post you create, you generate more chances for your target market to find you.

In addition to its SEO benefits, having a blog humanizes your brand. By sharing with readers your passions and interests, you are giving them a face to associate with your business. Everyone is more easily persuaded when the person doing the convincing is likeable. In reflecting your charming personality through your blog posts, you are increasing the chances of turning your site visitors into clients.

The third most important benefit DeMers touched on in his article is that blogging builds industry authority. In creating content that relates to your industry or business, you are showcasing your expertise in that area. Human nature dictates that we trust whom we believe to be experts, and in sharing your insights, you are asserting that you indeed are one. It is for this exact reason that top professional bloggers often collaborate with large companies or create their own lines of specialty products. Companies recognize that blog readers trust and value their blogger's opinion, so when a new product is endorsed by them, the reader assumes the product's quality and importance based on the trust they've developed for the blogger.

Blogging encompasses few parameters, which makes it a popular social media choice. It's *your* blog so *you* get to choose the content! While this means that you have the freedom to blog about whatever your heart desires, it is a smart business move to find a subject matter related to your industry that you're knowledgeable and passionate about.

For example, an online boutique might create a fashion blog to highlight new arrivals and drive visitors to their store. Similarly, an online marketing agency would do well to write blog posts outlining tips for using Google Adwords and SEO.

What are you waiting for? This is your opportunity to connect with potential customers without trying to sell. It gives them a personal connection that harbours brand loyalty. Loyal customers are more inclined to be repeat customers, making this essential step in creating your online reputation, undoubtedly important.

As with anything posted online though, you must be careful of the content tone and timing of your blogs particularly if related to your business or brand. This next case-study of reputation ruin came from a company who made a comment at *absolutely* the wrong time.

Reputation Wrecking Ball

Tweeting During Tragedy

It's important for brands to stay on top of what's going on in the media to stay relevant; however, it's not always appropriate for the business to comment on a story or event. One of the biggest social media blunders from big brands is using tragic events to promote and monetize. All too often, we see large companies make this mistake:

In 2011, during the protests in Egypt, the Kenneth Cole Twitter account tweeted: "Millions are in uproar in #Cairo. Rumor is they heard our new spring collection is now available." (Buzzfeed, 2011). There were no doubts that the account manager meant any harm by the comment, but the insensitive tweet offended most of Twitter.

Similarly, sometimes a company means well and wishes to pay its respects to those involved in the tragedy. When Kmart tweeted "Our thoughts and prayers are with the victims of this terrible tragedy" shortly after the Newtown shootings, its audience saw sincerity from the brand. It wasn't until people started to notice that the account had added a promotional hashtag, #Fab15Toys, to the tweet, that the brand began to receive backlash.

Lastly, we must heavily consider appropriate timing before posting. Just a few hours after the Aurora shooting, the North American Rifleman Association posted "Good morning, shooters. Happy Friday! Weekend plans?" What was sure to be a scheduled tweet was posted at an inappropriate time and offended most of America (Buzzfeed, 2011).

To avoid being the target of social media scrutiny, carefully construct all content you post and share during the time surrounding the events. It's generally a good rule to ask yourself "If an immediate family member were struck by this tragedy, would I want them to see this post?" If the post is making light of the situation, promotional in any way, or has a hashtag or direct reference to your brand, the answer is likely "no."

Step 7. Get in the Press

Now that you have your online presence visible and in full control with a frequently updated blog, look for opportunities for even greater exposure. If you play your cards right, the media can be a valuable tool in growing your business. There are countless opportunities for you to create that can result in press attention. Here are a few:

Popular websites that feature multiple writers are always looking for additional content. Sites such as Buzzfeed.com and About.com are excellent examples of webpages that compile countless content from multiple columnists. Try reaching out to these websites that fit into your niche, and ask your target audience to feature you as a guest blogger. Although you may not be compensated directly by the website, you will reap the benefits of having this blog linked to your very own. By merely including your website in the tagline, a significant amount of attention will generate back to your domain.

Another way to garner attention from the press is to look for opportunities to be interviewed. Reach out to a popular columnist with an idea for a story in an area of which you are an expert in. Once again, ask him or her to link back to your website and ensure your name or brand are mentioned throughout the article.

As always, be professional when working with media and take care in the message you are sending. This is your first impression to many new, potential clients. It might take time and some work, but when executed correctly, media appearances can be invaluable for generating leads.

Completing and expanding on these seven steps, will jumpstart an ever-valuable, positive online reputation.

How to Outshine the Competition

In the online world in which competition is not limited by geography, first impressions are everything. Feedback, ratings, and reviews are the fastest ways for you to garner the trust and respect of clients. Consumers have so much choice, which makes it even more important for

you to stand out from your market's competitors. More often than not, customers are more likely to leave negative feedback versus positive feedback. When one bad review can outshine dozens of 5-star praises, it's important to collect as much positive feedback as possible. Here's how you can encourage your (satisfied) clients to leave reviews:

a. **Follow up with** all clients by email, phone, or in person to ask about their experiences. If their experience was a positive one, kindly ask them to leave you a review online. Some outlets you may choose to collect reviews on might include your Facebook Page, TripAdvisor, Yelp, Consumer Reports, and Google or Yahoo listings. If the experiences your customers or clients have shared are negative, it is wonderful that you uncovered those before they start speaking to others. Ask them how you can make it right.

After you've taken steps to turn their experience around, ask them then if they might write you a review. This may seem risky, but if they detail their experience, others will appreciate that you went above and beyond to correct the issue. This will give future customers peace of mind that your intention is to provide excellent service and you will follow through responsibly and take care of them if the situation arises.

b. **Don't just leave** the glowing remarks of happy customers on review sites. Rather, flaunt them where the action is on your website! It's simple to add a reviews section that will display the testimonials. Consider adding a contact box on the page as a way for customers to express their views easily, right on your website.

c. **Customers don't want** to take much time out of their day to leave you a review. If you make it simple for them and streamline the process, you will collect significantly more responses. Many review websites have a tool that will allow you to input customer email addresses, and the website will send out an invitation to leave feedback. Another way to make it easy for your customers is by creating a QR code or bitly link so that your review destination is easy to find. From there, add the link to your business cards, packing slips, receipts, invoices, or any other objects your clients receive upon making a purchase. The goal is to make it *too* easy review.

d. **Negative feedback is** almost a guarantee in the world of business. No matter how careful you are and how hard you try to please, someone out there will have expectations that you just couldn't meet (or didn't know you were supposed to!). Quite often these clients won't even communicate their displeasure with you and will take it straight to a review site. The upside of many of these sites is that they allow responses from business owners or managers. It may be difficult to not get defensive and tear down the client, but consider the recipient of your response. Is it for that one client who likely won't be pleased enough at this point to return? Or, is it for the potential customers who are looking at your ratings? Don't play into the negative tones of the bad review. Rather, write what potential clients want to hear: own up, apologize, provide an explanation, offer a course of action to rectify, apologize once more, and thank the reviewer for his or her honest feedback. Yes, it may be difficult and you might be gritting your teeth throughout the entire response, but the last thing potential customers want to see is you berating another customer for their bad experience that, presumably, *you* were responsible for.

e. **Motivation is the** factor that compels us to do something, and as mentioned, there's little motivation for a customer to leave a review. In order to collect plenty of reviews, especially when just starting out, consider creating an incentive for the customer. Have you ever shopped at a store, and upon being handed the receipt, the cashier points to a survey link at the bottom of the slip where you can answer a short survey and receive X amount off your next purchase? Large retailers such as Starbucks are infamous for doing this as a method of quality control.

By simply offering clients a percentage saved from further business or a small gift card to a local coffee shop, you are not only gathering valuable reviews, but also establishing future business from that client. If you follow these methods and practice them frequently, glowing ratings will start to pour in.

To summarize: "Create your own domain, establish a clear, fleshed-out presence on multiple social networking sites, post to each of them at least once a month and keep monitoring the Web for unflattering photos or mentions. If they come up, do your best to bury them with positive content" (Adams, 2013). Always be aware, active, and pre-emptive in all of your online efforts.

The Corporate Shift
to See-Through

*The value of being connected
and transparent is so high that
the road-bumps of privacy issues
are much lower in actual experience
than people's fears.*

–Reid Hoffman

One of the biggest corporate shifts of the 21st century has been the move to more environmentally and socially responsible companies. A large part of the movement emphasizing corporate social responsibility is creating business transparency so that consumers are fully aware of the way the company conducts themselves and can therefore make an informed purchasing decision. Increasingly, brands large and small alike are "opening up" publicly.

Transparency is becoming a new rule in business, one aspect of which dictates how open companies are to criticism. These businesses value feedback and have developed a customized communication strategy that adds a human touch. Companies practicing transparency believe in an "honesty is the best policy" approach; if consumers view them as a brand that keeps no secrets from customers, they can trust their honesty which creates a more appealing brand image.

How transparent do they decide to go? Some common practices of transparency in businesses are:

- Keeping no secrets. Transparency aims to address problems publicly, even if it makes that business appear unfavourable.

- Developing a unique one-to-one communication channel. This gives customers a way to address their concerns and rest assured that their voices will be heard.

- Feedback request. In requesting feedback, these companies are welcoming constructive criticism and showing customers that their opinions matter.

- Providing transparency for customers to openly discuss your products or services.

Be aware that transparency can be tricky. Effectively, you are being 100% open with your customers, and allowing them to publicly leave you feedback and criticize your company. In other words, you have to be prepared for the worst while hoping for the best and understand how to spin each situation in your favour. Yet, if you're not being transparent at all, you're running an even bigger risk of being seen as untrustworthy.

While both options may have their challenges, it is always best to choose transparency over avoiding something and covering up. If you need further convincing, look to the next chapter for prize examples of poor initiatives.

Biggest Transparency Failures

Dark Horse Café

Dark Horse Café is a small chain of coffee shops in Toronto, Canada. They pride themselves on delivering true espresso in a Starbucks-saturated landscape and appeal to alternative crowds and those who prefer to support small-businesses. Recently, the Dark Horse Café was the target of unwanted media attention after it received a critical tweet from a customer. The criticism wasn't overly harsh and simply complained about the lack of electrical outlets in the café, making it difficult for patrons who wished to work on their laptops. Most customers would hardly blink an eye seeing a tweet like this from a fellow coffee drinker and it certainly wouldn't stop most from visiting Dark Horse Café. What makes this situation interesting is how the coffee shop responded:

https://twitter.com/darkhorsecafe/status/7801863504

"@aprildunford that's awesome…we are in the coffee business, not the office business. We have plenty of outlets to do what we need."

Obviously, it is very clear what they did wrong. The online world doesn't appreciate this kind of passive/aggressive behavior, and it was quickly shared throughout social networks. What Dark Horse Café seemed to have forgotten when crafting their reply, is that this critic was a *customer* and should therefore be treated with respect. In addition, their public response would be seen by a huge portion of their loyal customer base – those that follow their social media.

Frustrated by the poor response, fellow customers spread the tweet across many blogs and websites, garnering it a lot of negative attention.

Have you ever heard the phrase "if someone will discuss others with you, they will certainly discuss you with others?" This saying can be applied to this scenario and the assumption was: if they openly treat a customer this poorly, they will certainly treat their other customers the same way.

Amy's Baking Company

Do you remember those great review sites we discussed in the previous chapter? At some point, it is almost inevitable for every business to receive a negative review. For Amy's Baking Company, this was no exception.

The small American bistro received quite a bit of media attention after the owner became fed up with seeing consistently low-rated Yelp reviews and started to make rude replies to the detractors. There are far too many responses to quote, but many included disrespectful language such as "moron," "ugly," "loser," telling customers to "be quiet!!!" and accusing many of "lying" about having eaten at their restaurant (Laudig, 2010). This was picked up by the local news, spreading the embarrassment further.

While it may not always be easy, it's critical for business owners to be polite, put their emotions aside, and ask how they can compensate or help. Needless to say, Amy's Baking Company is no longer in business.

Nestlé

Due to the fact that Dark Horse Café and Amy's Baking Company are both small, local businesses, you might think it's easy for companies of this size to slip up once in awhile. After all, it's often the owner or other employee with little experience who are in-charge of social media, unlike the PR professionals that handle big business platforms.

Nestlé, one of the world's largest food industry tycoons, recently showed us how easy it is for even the professionals to mess up.

A few years ago, environmental activists left negative comments on Nestlé's Facebook page, criticising their use of palm oil in their products and the deforestation, greenhouse gas emitting, and species endangering effects that it has. Several more activists jumped in, creating momentum, until the company's entire Facebook page was full of critical comments and cries for change.

Rather than choosing to openly address the concerns and critiques of this large group of individuals, Nestlé chose to shut down their Facebook and social media accounts. It seems that someone in charge wrongly assumed that if he or she took away the activists' platform, the virtual rioting would cease and there would be no need to address it. However, rather than taking responsibility and addressing the public scrutiny, the food giant's actions made the silent statement that they are not a company that wants to hear of, nor cares about, issues from its customer base. The important lesson in this case is that avoiding criticism and acting like "it's not there" isn't going to make it go away (McCarthy, 2010).

The most frustrating thing in each of these cases is that all instances were so easily avoidable! Would these events have escalated had Dark House Café courteously replied to the outlet issue with "Our apologies for not being more accommodating to those with laptops. We will consider ways in which we can change this. Thanks!?" What if the owner of Amy's Baking Company chose to keep her cool and calmly apologize before inviting the guest back for a better dining experience? How about if Nestlé had simply acknowledged the concern of the activists, assured the public they were an environmentally responsible company, and say that they are discussing alternative options? Clearly, they would have avoided their mess. These examples, and countless others, go to show that practicing business transparency and respecting your customers in your replies, are crucial for reputation and success.

Reputation Bombs

In the digital era, nothing is protecting you from criticism anymore. This is good from a freedom of speech perspective; bad if your company has been defamed and attacked.

–Dan Virgillito

Online reputation bombs are exactly how they sound – severely devastating and not leaving much left behind after them. They come in various shapes and sizes and leave different levels of damage. No matter the kind or size of the "bomb" though, the damage is always deep and reversing its impact can be a long and exhaustive process. Once in awhile, a brand, company, or person experiences a bomb so devastating that the damages are irreversible.

Can you think of an example of a reputation bomb? One such type is complaints on social media that we discussed in previous chapters. The negligent actions of each company's representatives in those cases caused the bomb to drop and forced the business to take necessary action to reverse the damage and restore its reputation. In the case of Amy's Baking Company, the bomb was so devastating that destruction could not be reversed and the restaurant was forced to close its doors. By taking appropriate measures and addressing your customers directly in a polite and respectful manner, these complaints shouldn't pose a huge threat.

We discussed the bomb that's dropped as a result of companies being negligent to complaints in previous detail, so you already know to avoid that catastrophe. You know what *not* to do if you find yourself in that position and the measures you can take to save your reputation when faced with a negative review. The thing is though, this kind of bomb is rarely even *that* severe in comparison to the true reputation ruiners.

I'm sure you're wondering: how do they get any worse that that? Negative comments on review platforms get buried quickly by reviews from (hopefully) happy customers. Luckily, the upside of social media is that everything happens so quick that it doesn't take long before people are focusing on something else.

The catch is that the customers who have complaints that *really* want to hit you hard don't focus solely on a few negative reviews. The serious reputation bombs show up in search engines. That's exactly what makes them so powerful. This negative content that shows up on search engines can come in different forms. Let's take a look…

Negative Reviews

We discussed sites like Yelp and TripAdvisor, but would you believe that there are entire websites dedicated solely to negative reviews? Rather than regular review sites in which customer leave honest reviews noting pros and cons, these websites are strictly negative content. Such sites, like Ripoff Report and Pissed Consumer, are a melting pot of angry customers.

These negative review sites hit hard because they often show up high in search results and there are no positive reviews on the site to outshine the negative ones. Those who post on such websites are out to get "justice" and feel that ruining the company's or person's reputation is the best way to serve it.

Keep in mind that 70% of consumers trust a company with at least 6 to 10 good reviews. (Dialog Marketing, 2012). On the flipside, even just one negative review will cause consumers to shy away from the business. Clearly, you can see the power of social media and the strength of these online reviews.

Hate Sites

While negative review sites seem extreme, they're fairly tame in comparison to other reputation bombs. For some people, leaving a bad review for others to see is simply not enough. For whatever reason, these individuals are ready to spend a good deal of time and effort in order to ruin a company's reputation.

Hate sites are entire domains dedicated to the defamation of a business, or person's name. Such sites are packed with negative content, often much of which is construed, and use harsh words to insult brands and individuals. While there are some legal steps that can be taken to pull down these sites, the damage is usually done by the time the legal process has a chance to take action. If a hate site manages to creep its way to the top of search engines results, potential clients will see it as a huge red flag and choose not to conduct business with you.

A fantastic example of a hate site leading to a ruined reputation was acted out in the long-running sitcom, "How I Met Your Mother." In one particular episode, the show's main character, Ted, discovers that a spiteful ex-girlfriend created a hate website dedicated to him – TedMosbyIsAJerk.com. After typing his name into Google, he sees that it is the first website to pop up and its traffic counter had seen almost half a million visitors. While this example may be a fictional (and humorous) one, the fact remains that there are a special, select bunch of people who will go that extra mile to destroy your reputation.

Unfortunately, easy access to hate sites are a popular method for them to achieve this.

Anonymous Forums

Anonymity seems to empower many individuals to say what they would not deem appropriate to say if their identity were known. Platforms with no transparency welcome tactless comments, lies, and cyber-bullying. The privacy policies of many of these anonymous apps and websites make it nearly impossible to track down the original poster, so it's even more crucial to be aware that these websites exist.

One particular app, Yik Yak, garnered a lot of media attention for enabling the perfect environment for cyber-bullying and harassment. The open-forum app allows conversation between individuals within a 5-mile radius and all identities of posters are hidden (Schauer, 2015).

To most, the 5-mile radius limitation makes the app purposeless, but Yik Yak is creating a lot of problems for high schools and college campuses. While there have been no stories of Yik Yak conversations posing threats to any brands, this environment has enabled the harassment of countless individuals.

As we put our brands and ourselves out there to the public, it's important to be aware of websites and forums, anonymous or not, that pose a potential threat to our reputations. Other popular anonymous forum websites and apps include Whisper, Secret, Reddit, Big Old Soapbox, and Office Leaks. It never hurts to perform a quick name or company search on these websites once in awhile to ensure that you haven't found yourself the target of the always-feared 'Mr/s. Anonymous.'

Negative Media

Media outlets have nearly a limitless reach. One news website may pick up a story and suddenly three television stations are running it. Media attention can have a snowball effect which means that negative public coverage often has a devastating effect on brands. Whether it's print, TV, or online media; the damage caused by the bad press can shut down a business.

While there are so many examples of this type of devastation to choose from, let's take a look at how negative media attention dropped a reputation bomb on a popular global clothing brand, American Apparel. For years, American Apparel has been a target for media scrutiny because of its inappropriate, and often offensive, hyper-sexualized advertisements. Almost on a monthly basis for years, there was another racy ad of theirs garnering media attention. If you type "American Apparel" into Google, all of the results following the store's actual website are various news stories, which are full of criticism and negative attention. While the clothing store has not identified that it will be shutting down, the brand has closed the doors on a great deal of its retail stores, pulled back on production, and laid off countless employees (Neate, 2015).

As you can see, reputation bombs are aptly named as they often cause real damage. These bombs explode on businesses and individuals, hitting them where it hurts. They are not to be taken lightly, and it is imperative to perform damage control before they can get to this point.

Stop the Bleeding

*The goal is to get back to business as usual
and get the whole issue off the table.*

–Dan Millar

Crisis management might be the single most important element
in restoring a damaged online reputation. No matter the magnitude
– whether a large publication broadcasted negative content about your
company, or you are simply the target for a parade of rude tweets and
blog posts – almost any kind of negative content can cause damage
to your online (and offline) reputation. While the destruction can
be devastating, there are often ways to avoid and reverse such charges.

As is with most cases of damage control, the first step to take
is to prevent the problem from escalating to the point of no return.
It is necessary to always be aware of how anything posted online
may be seen or construed by various
audiences. The world is made up
of all kinds of types, and what may
be funny or playful to some, might
be offensive and inexcusable to
others. It is important to ensure
your content is politically correct,
non-aggressive, and could never
be manipulated to look like an attack
on a person or group of people. Be sure to keep every social
media account your company, and you personally, have as neutral
and politically correct as possible. Rather than jumping on trends,
("Everyone is using this hashtag with mild political undertones
so I should too!") only post what will highlight your business
in a positive light.

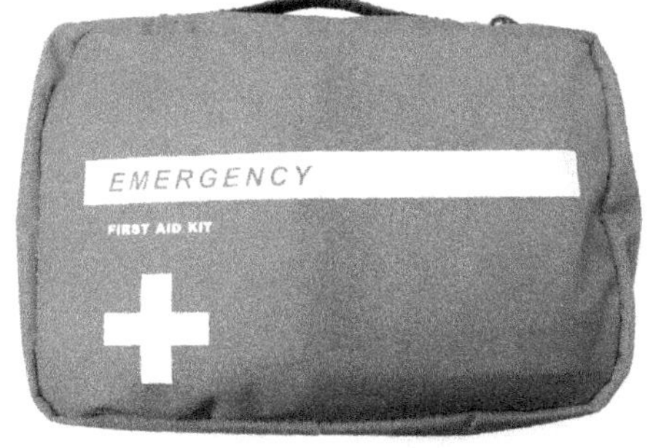

Of course, we are all human and we sometimes slip up. None of the previous examples of poor reputation management *intended* harm or to welcome a wrath of negative online attention; it was simply an error in judgement that spiraled out of control. Luckily, there are some steps to reverse the damage caused by a reputation bomb:

Monitor the Damage

Do you remember those Google Alerts and name-search tools we discussed in earlier chapters? Those tools really come in handy in these situations. The first step in rebuilding your online reputation is taking control and discovering all of the threats and damages. When a crisis hits, you cannot take action without careful evaluation. Unearth the negative content and carefully monitor any new posts. When you are fully aware of the damages, you can start to assess the situation and develop recovery strategies.

Communicate

In the online world, we are well aware that things happen within a blink of an eye. That being said, your online reputation can be harmed instantly. Because everything online happens in real time, you need to think fast and provide quick answers to any concerned customers. Communicating promptly during a crisis is a very important first step in recovering and maintaining your online reputation. Your customers will appreciate that you are responsive, taking any concerns they have seriously, and that you are still around to resolve the issues. Businesses that are unresponsive in these fight-or-flight scenarios lose the respect of their customers and further damage their reputation.

Aggressive SEO

Did you know that what the first and second page of Google say about you is more important than your business card? Websites with higher ranks make it on the first pages of Google and display information about you. If negative or false content is published, you have to do your best and set up an online reputation management strategy to bury these results. To do this, begin by brushing up on SEO and aggressively work to publish content that will show up higher in search results.

Typically, social media accounts will pop up as some of the first results, so ensure that all of your accounts are actively set up. Consider creating accounts on platforms that you are not currently on to create more opportunities to appear higher than the negative results. If you have a friend who has a strong online presence with a good reputation, ask him or her if he or she would do you a favour and create content about you and your business.

While creating additional content can be effective by out-ranking the negative results, ensure that you are still thoughtful in what you are posting. When implementing this strategy, it's important to never appear spammy to those who are still engaging with you. Be careful not to do more damage and create a mountain out of a molehill.

Removing False Reviews

Some of the best news for businesses is that many online reviews, under certain circumstances, can be removed by the review website. If the review is false or harmful, it can be taken down by the host website. These sites take honesty and objective consumer opinions very seriously; therefore, you must be able to prove that the review is false and defamatory. Generally, the victim of the review will pursue the author in a legal environment. From there, a subpoena plan is then sent to the review site by the victim, requesting that the negative content be removed. Various websites have their own policies for taking down content and offering advice on different legal measures, so be sure to check with the individual site to see if you have a case.

Hiring a Skilled Investigator

If someone is anonymous and posted negative statements about you
or your brand, how do you find the culprit? Well, usually these types
of anonymous posters hide their IP addresses with a free easy to use
tool called Tor. It takes a person who is skilled in this area to find the
poster's information. Cyber threats are common and have created an
entire industry of professionals who specialize in finding your attacker.
If severe damage has been done to your brand image, an effective
solution is to hire a skilled analyst to investigate your attackers
and find the origin of trouble through tracing email, data indexing,
and other sources.

The adultery "dating" website, Ashley Madison, was victim to
a cyber-attack that shook the digital world. Data from 37 million
members was leaked by an anonymous hacking crew known as
The Impact Team. After several weeks of threats, the team posted
the recovered files incriminating all users of the site. The list contained
hundreds of recognizable names from politicians to television stars,

damaging millions of reputations. While Ashley Madison was charging members monthly to delete data from the system, the hackers revealed that the data was not being erased at all. Currently, the company is facing a $578 million class action lawsuit and several of its famous members are the target for non-stop media attacks (Noronha, 2015).

While many hackers are regarded as crooks seeking financial gain, there are those that are extortionists, working hard to shut down entire businesses and organizations. The Impact Team was driven by moral outrage as opposed to seeking financial gain. Such organizations that offer services that are taboo, politically incorrect, or morally debated, should always be prepared for cyber attacks.

Be Social

Utilize your brand's social media accounts so they may reach their full potential. While these accounts may seem high maintenance – and they are – actively updating your social media has a strong impact. Step up your online presence and work hard to make it shine. Keep in mind that some social media platforms have more benefits than others. The most powerful social media networks that the majority use are: Twitter, LinkedIn, Instagram, Facebook, Google+, YouTube, and Pinterest. Don't forget to link them all together and include your website in your profile whenever possible.

When using these platforms, try thinking outside the box. You can make YouTube videos that better describe your services to your clients and share those videos on social media. Google, as well as other search engines, rank videos highly, making creating and sharing them an online reputation tactic that is worth gold.

Updating your blog with fresh content and posting regularly will strengthen its impact in search results and increase your online presence. By blogging, you can emphasize your brand's value and strengths. All you need is to buy a domain name (which was previously

explained) with your brand's name and create a professional
online presence that is filled with informative content. Try updating
it with information regarding your services, trends in your industry,
and simple advice on how your services can benefit readers. Blogging
drives traffic which helps you build leads. Most importantly, blogging
creates a personal connection with your readers and customers.
In building trust and making that connection, you are decreasing
the effect that any reputation bombs have.

A Strong PR Campaign

As stated previously, press coverage is an important step in building
your online reputation. I'm mentioning the media again because
it is also a vital tool for recovering a damaged reputation. A strong and
active PR campaign doesn't necessarily mean the usual company press
releases. Do a bit of research and find interesting ways to promote your
business. Consider sponsoring an event that is related to your industry.
Perhaps you can offer to speak at a local lecture or presentation in
which you would be regarded as an expert. Get creative and brainstorm
ways in which you can seek positive media attention that will stand out
from the crowd. All of this positive coverage from trusted sources
will begin to outweigh the negative attention.

Here's a Win-Win

> *When you incorporate giving into your
> business in an authentic and transparent
> way, your customers become your
> best marketers.*
>
> —BLAKE MYCOSKIE

Philanthropic pursuits benefit everyone involved. While we should
always involve ourselves with philanthropic work with sincerity to
fight for a cause, a byproduct of this volunteering and sponsoring

not-for-profit organizations is that it also repairs and enhances
your reputation.

When performed genuinely, philanthropy has helped restore
countless corporate reputations and reflects a sense of humanity and
social responsibility on the participating company. Almost every major
organization has tied itself to at least one cause; it's smart for small
businesses and individuals to do the same. Choose a cause that you
really believe in, because that passion will shine through and make
your efforts feel genuine for both yourself and potential clients.

Aside from benefiting the community and performing good deeds,
one of the best aspects of philanthropy is that it is accessible for anyone
and any budget. While sponsoring large charity events or making
substantial donations is wonderful, if your budget doesn't quite allow
for that, donating your time and volunteering is just as appreciated.
If you're not in a place yet that you can run a donation-matching
campaign, consider volunteering to collect donations instead. If your
budget doesn't have room for a title sponsorship at an event, volunteer
your time at the event. Find a cause, or a couple of causes, that you feel
passionate about and lend yourself in whichever capacity you can.

Be Remarkable

Taking special care in delivering remarkable customer service is the
most impactful way to restore your online reputation. When your main
focus is providing outstanding service, your customers will be happy
and feel taken care of. Encourage these happy customers to add their
reviews to websites. An outpour of positive reviews will start to push
down the poor ones. Most importantly though, in providing great
customer service, you are instilling trust in your current customers
while taking preventative measures to avoid a damaged reputation
in the future.

You're probably wondering how one person can manage all of these aspects of damage control? The truth is, it's incredibly hard, time-consuming, and nearly impossible for one individual to carry out. If you find yourself the target of a damaged online reputation, the chances are high that you are feeling hurt, victimized, and not at your best. Rather than taking on the responsibility of having to juggle managing public relations campaigns, content development, social media and blog updates, and monitoring activity, consider handing the task over to a professional.

While most companies or individuals don't have experience in running online reputation campaigns and don't have the training required, there are entire firms that exist to do just that. An experienced reputation management firm can consult, assess, and strategize the most effective way to fix your reputation. Employees of these firms are experts in content production, promotion, social media strategies, and public relations. With their help and careful execution, you can rest assured that your reputation and its restoration are in good hands.

Understanding Branding

In the world of online business, your brand is your livelihood. Branding is how customers separate you from the thousands of others who are in the same business and offer the same services that you do. Branding allows audiences to immediately recognize you because of the distinction it creates. Ultimately, your brand is what forms and facilitates that connection with your clients.

A brand runs a lot deeper than a mere logo, catch phrase, or design that distinguishes a particular product or service. Often, modern marketers aim to create an experience and provoke emotions in an effort to create an attachment to the brand. The goal is to have a brand that's well-known, has a loyal following, and is easily recognizable, building brand equity.

Many cases of online reputation damage occur because individuals, businesses, or even large organizations, do not properly manage the information that describes them. This general information available about your business should reflect your identity and form your brand. Without taking the time and care to carefully create your brand, others will do it for you, leaving you out of control of your public identity.

This all rings true to personal branding, too. Personal branding is the most important step in managing your reputation. It is what ties everything we've learned together. Your personal brand reflects your values, your worth, and the image you wish to portray. Superior personal branding will emphasize what makes you different and will set you apart from your competitors. A strong personal brand presence dilutes the impact of negative feedback and helps preserve your quality reputation.

In this chapter, you will not only learn the importance of your brand, but how to develop your brand identity, construct your image, and successfully manage your brand.

Creating Your Brand

As we discussed, the objective in creating a brand is to set yourself apart from "the rest." To avoid blending in with the others with similar skills, we must delve into what makes you stand out.

Lida Citroen, for Social Media Today, says: "The foundation of personal branding rests on authenticity: The ability to tap into your genuine, humble, and individual human qualities from which your identity, personality, and character stem" (Citroen, 2014).

Using this philosophy as a guide, we will now take a look at a comprehensive series of steps to help you identify your brand.

Step 1. Mindful of Motivation

What motivates you? What makes you get out of bed every morning to seize the day? What really inspires you? At the heart of the answer to these questions are your values. These standards of behaviour guide your actions and determine your judgement of what is important in life. Often, your values are the first thing you consider when making a choice or choosing a path.

It is important for clients to understand the values of the business they are supporting. While they might not always agree with your set of values, customers appreciate knowing what guides your decisions as it determines how you conduct business. For your customers and yourself, it is important for your brand to convey your set of values.

To get to the root of your priorities and discover your values, consider:

- What things are important in the way you work and live?

- How do you measure your personal and professional success?

- What are your main priorities?

- When were you the happiest? Who were you with and what were you doing?

- When were you the most proud? What factors contribute to this?

- What makes you feel fulfilled?

Your list of values may look something like this (or entirely
different – that's okay!):

- Family

- Intelligence

- Ambition

- Creativity

- Compassion

- Honesty

Step 2. Lose the Lengthy List

Once you begin creating a list of values that guide your life and
decisions, you might find yourself with a lengthy list. We're all complex
individuals and what drives us may vary day to day and year to year.
For instance, family may be one of your values, but upon learning of
a new internal position that will soon come available at your company,
you've chosen to go on the voluntary weekend corporate trip because
you also value advancement and growth. This doesn't mean that you
are throwing your family values out the window. It's all about balancing
and prioritizing your values.

Your list is composed of values that each affect your drive in some
way. A few of those values though, will drive you *more* than the others.
Your values aren't equal so it is important to prioritize them effectively
and as best as you can. This step is one with a lot of self-reflection and
you will have to dig deep inside yourself. It's probably the most difficult
one as you find yourself weighing two things that are important to you
that satisfy different areas of your life.

You may choose to prioritize in whatever way makes sense for you,
but selecting your Top 5 is a good place to start. Remember, the goal

of your personal brand is not just about growing professionally, increasing sales, and attracting new clients, but rather about being happy with the path of your professional career.

Here are a few guiding steps to help you in the prioritizing process:

- Write out a list, in no special order, of no more than 20 of your personal values

- Starting with the first two, begin comparing sets of values and determining which is more important. Ask yourself which of these values you would satisfy if you could only satisfy one. It might help to envision a scenario that you would find yourself making a choice. For example: going back to the family versus corporate trip scenario, which would you choose if it were a loved one's birthday?

- Once you've determined which value is more important, strike out the other. If you can't choose between either, consider them tied for now as we work through the list.

- Continue through until your list consists of five values and are ranked in order. Check these top priorities and ensure that they emulate the vision you have for yourself and your career.

Prioritizing your values will help in decision making. Additionally, it will relay your sense of integrity and how you approach business with your clients.

Step 3. Wave a Magic Wand

In addition to your personal set of values, your passions make up a lot of who you are. At its core, your brand is your essence so it is important to capture your passions in addition to your values. What is it that you wish you could spend most of your time doing? Your answers to this question are your passions. Your passions give you a deep sense of purpose and self-satisfaction, and are what you choose to invest your time, money, and heart into, simply for the sake of fulfilling it.

Your passions are just as important as your values when it comes to creating your personal brand. Alike to your values, your passions steer your life, but in the direction of your dreams. In revealing your passions, you will begin to see the creation of your personal brand.

Sometimes though, our passions are not always clear. To delve deep into what you're truly happy doing, consider this: if you won billions of dollars and had near-limitless funds so that you were comfortably living off the interest, what would you get up to do every day? Yes, we all have a list of our lottery fantasies like traveling the world, creating a charity, and taking care of every family member, but *after* you've done all of those things what would you do? The answers to this question will reveal your passions.

Step 4: Your Personality Makeup

Let's continue to look at what shapes you in our discovery of your personal brand. Your traits are like the genetic makeup of your personality. Traits are unique to you, shaping you as a human being, which is why they are essential in defining a brand that sets you apart from the rest.

According to Allison Mooney, author of Pressing The Right Buttons, we are often a *blend* of personality types rather than strictly just one. It is important to the success of your business, career (and relationships!) however to understand which type you best fit. In this way we can appreciate and respect each other's differences and know how to work to our strengths (Mooney, 2007).

There are many different tests, theories, and exercises that will help define your personal set of traits.

- Gordon Allport's Trait Theory categorizes personality traits into three levels – Cardinal Traits, Central Traits, and Secondary Traits – based on how much they dominate an individual's personality.

- Psychologist Hans Eysenck created the Three Dimensions of Personality theory based upon what he believes to be three universal traits and which side of the spectrum people fall on for those traits. Eysenck's three determining traits are: Introversion-Extraversion, Neuroticism-Emotional Stability, and degree of Psychoticism.

- Based on the Three Dimensions of Personality theory and others, the most widely accepted way to determine personality traits is The Big Five: Five-Factor Model. This model theorizes that there are five core traits and the varying degrees of which a person possesses each determines that individual's personality.

If we look at The Big Five theory, we can self-asses the degree to which we possess each of the dominating traits. Take a look at these traits and determine where you fall on the scale of: extraversion, agreeableness, openness to experience, conscientiousness, and neuroticism. For the most candid and honest response, consider taking one of the thousands of personality tests offered online. Remember, there is no right or wrong answer when identifying your traits, it is simply a way to help develop and shape your personal brand (Mooney, 2007).

Step 5: Are You Seeing Straight?

Once you've defined your core values, discovered your passions,
and identified your personality traits, you can evaluate and discuss
your findings. We all have a perception of ourselves that varies slightly
from how others see us, so it is helpful to get other opinions. Ask your
family, close friends, and colleagues what they think your identifying
attributes are. Those who see you professionally may have a different
set of answers than those who are close to you on a more personal
level. Consider the outside input and take note of any answers that
are the most popular among those you've asked.

Your brand isn't built on who *you* think you are, but rather, how others
perceive you. Understanding what defining characteristics you emulate
to others will assist in developing your personal brand.

Now that you've compiled a list of your values, passions, and traits,
you have the foundation for your personal brand. These attributes are
what set you apart from others and what will guide everything you do.
You will want to be completely satisfied with the list, because every
online move you make should reflect these; they're the foundation
for which you will be recognized. Through social media, your website,
portfolio, and other marketing tools, we will begin to form the brand
image that you've created.

Build a Brand with These Tools

–John Morgan

You should now have a general idea of what your personal brand is and what you will be conveying to the online (and offline) world. In business, we use a variety of marketing elements to be seen and remembered by our clients. The next step in creating your personal brand is rebranding each of those marketing tools to unify your vision. It is through these tools that the world will see who you are and what you're about. When setting up these tools, remember to be conscious of the message they are sending and how that aligns with your brand.

Step 1: No More Selfies

Having professional headshots taken for social media and your online platforms are both a necessity and an investment when building your online reputation and creating your brand. Too often I see individuals making the mistake of using a selfie or a headshot cropped from a group photo of an obvious night out with friends as their default photo on social media. Neither of these photos, as flattering as they may be, convey the professionalism and confidence that you should want in a profile photo.

A professional headshot photo is a vital component of your marketing toolkit and will carry one of the longest lasting impacts. This is how your clients will recognize you and visualize you as you connect. Yes, a professional photography session can get quite expensive, but it is well worth the investment. The photographer understands how to manage lighting and maximize on your features to create a commanding image. Your session not only includes taking the photos, but also the time the photographer will take to edit the photos, which will create a professional image.

Once you have your professional headshots, it is important to stay consistent with your photos. Keep them up to date so that you're always recognizable and be sure to use the same image across all platforms for unity. Pick that one favorite photo that imitates your inner executive. Make this photo your default so that there is no confusion as to whether or not the attached work belongs to you.

Now that you have your image, where should you be using it? Everywhere. By posting your professional image frequently online, it triggers search engines to show these results when searching for your name or business. Your photos popping up in search results has the effect of reinforcing your recognizability and the added bonus of making any negative reviews or less-than-pleasant posts fall lower in rank. You should be placing your image on any author bios, social media profiles, blogs and guest blogging posts. For this to be effective, ensure that, upon receiving your edited photos, you change the generic file name to 'yourname.jpeg' or 'yourbusinessname.jpeg' so search engines can recognize it to pull it up for search results.

Step 2: Social Media on Steroids

Studies by Pew Research Center (2014) have shown that **74%** of all Internet users utilise social media so it is no wonder why this tool is deeply important in creating and unifying your brand. As discussed, there are countless platforms to choose from, so we will continue to focus on the ones that work best to support your brand and have users that fall into your target market. The audiences, benefits, and intricacies of the top platforms will be discussed in the chapter: Guide to Top Social Media Platforms.

After carefully
creating each of your
social media profiles, complete with
that professional headshot, you will
need to create value on your networks.
We want to ensure that everything we choose
to post and share reinforces our personal brand.
Don't only think of it as sharing content, but rather
imagine that you are curating a gallery full of photos, articles,
and words, that reflect your brand. Aaron Agius, a contributor to
Entrepreneur.com, advises to "Figure out which content is most likely
to gain visibility", but "Remember, humor can be difficult to pull off.
If you can use memes effectively, they can be powerful brand-building
tools. But if you aren't 100 percent sure how the audience will respond
to your image, resist the temptation" (Agius, 2015).

Step 3: Sent from my i-Phone

What sits at the end of your business correspondence is just as
important as the content of the message. This element is one that
is too often overlooked by professionals. Your email signature is
the final word on your email and the last impression that the reader
on the other end will have of you. Don't make the mistake of
undervaluing this tool.

Worse than having no email signature is having one that is definitely not professional. Most smartphones are pre-programmed with a default email signature such as "Sent from my iPhone." The issue with this is that the signature is acting as a marketing tool for *them*, the cellphone company, and not for you. Worse still than these generic signatures is having one that doesn't represent your brand. Don't make the mistake of thinking that quote you found which reads "Happiness is the key to success" will go over well with your clients.

That being said, what *should* you have in your email signature? You want to make sure that your signature allows those you're in contact with to connect with you even after the conversation. First and foremost, include your name, title, and company (if applicable) – this will show the world *who* you are. Then, show how to contact you: your website and telephone number. Lastly, leave them with how to connect with you further by creating icons that will link to your social media accounts. There are plenty of email building websites that can do this for you. Icons allow you to avoid using an excess of links to ensure that your signature doesn't begin to look cluttered and spammy.

Step 4: Making Movies

In addition to other social media platforms, YouTube is an ideal way to reinforce your brand and expand its reach. Creating videos does take time and effort. Few professionals choose to capitalize on creating scripts, filming, and edits due to the time commitment required. To really set your brand apart from the crowd, jump in and fill this gap! Establish yourself as an expert on a subject by creating short how-to videos to fill a particular niche.

For example, a real estate professional may choose to create a series of how to's such as "How to Buy Your First Home", or "How to Stage

Your House for a Quick Sale", etc. These videos are a great way to create wide-spread brand awareness as well as draw in new clients.

When making a title, the secret is to make sure your name or your business's name is in both the video title and in the video description. For extra SEO points, if that same name is in the file name of the video, you increase the chances of showing up in search engines.

President of Big Blue Robot Reputation Management Services, Dan Sorensen, spoke with Forbes's Cheryl Conner in 2014 regarding managing online reputation. He said to "encourage customers to show how they're using your product through YouTube videos. Videos tend to rank very well on Google and other search engines" (Conner, 2014).

Step 5: A Strategic Alliance

We see it all the time in the corporate world: two brands coming together in a partnership in an effort to expand their reach by way of a clever marketing strategy. Apple will only sell Beats by Dre headphones, Betty Crocker only uses Hershey brand mix-ins in their mixes, and even Disney has co-branded with several partners, most recently, Crocs. The thought behind this strategy is that tying your brand to another, well-established brand will expand your clientele and make you more established.

The concept of co-branding can be applied to benefit your personal brand by way of connecting with other reputable personal brands or organizations. Join a professional organization for those in your industry, or contribute to an alumni group you belong to. Creating guest posts for others in your professional network with blogs or media platforms is an effective way to spread your reach and make your presence known.

Step 6: Touchdowns and Downfalls

As with any aspect of business, proper management is essential for success; your personal brand is certainly no exception. Proper brand management ensures that you're enabling your brand to flourish and that you are in full control of defining it, rather than allowing it to define you.

Many reputation management experts agree on the one key to a business's or individual's growth, and that is consistency. Consistency paves the way for success and not only establishes a strong online reputation, but also accounts for credibility, relevance, measurement and keeps your brand's messages flowing through digital channels.

The skills of football players are revised constantly. Let's say we have two players; we'll call player one, Ian, and player two, Ton. Ian has shown unbeatable talent and has delivered remarkable goals. He also had downfalls, showing success in some games yet lacking follow-through in other ones. Ton on the other hand, may not have as much talent as Ian, but has scored on most of the games. Even though Ton's skills can't outshine Ian's, some executives would rather prefer keeping Ton. Why? Simply because he is consistent.

Many businesses would prefer an employee that leaves and arrives at the workplace at the same time every day. Clients have that same preference with the agent they choose to hire. The commitment they put into their work each day is constant which is appreciated by those invested. To really make your brand shine, show your consistency through regularly scheduled content. Keep your voice, topics, and quality of posts consistent.

While consistency is great in allowing those engaging with our brand to know what to expect, it doesn't help if we're consistently forgettable. The next key aspect of brand management is creating and maintaining memorable content.

There are countless approaches and ways to leave a mark and become memorable. In marketing your brand as one that's unique and original, you are sure to stand out from the crowd. How do you do this? Rather than merely using your platforms to show your experience and skills, take it up a notch! Consider ways in which you can provide your clients with solutions by doing things the competition isn't. Those how-to YouTube videos we discussed are a fabulous first step. Additionally, ensure that the content you're sharing isn't the same few stories that everyone else is posting, allowing viewers to keep scrolling past. Look for a gap in the niche and fill it!

These are simply some of the tools you can use for effective branding. As always, the key is consistency and constantly ensuring that all of your content and efforts lineup with the message and image of your personal brand. While there are countless ways to spread your reach, if the medium through which you're doing it doesn't line up with your brand, then it will do more harm than good.

Keeping Your Finger on the Pulse

What do people think of when they think about your brand? If the answer is nothing, or something other than you want it to be, than we have work to do.

–DETAVIO SAMUELS

If you don't use a tech tool to track your brand online, chances are that you'll waste your whole day struggling in front of the monitor. Tracking your online brand is essential in terms of monitoring to prevent any brand damage. They are also useful in keeping you notified of every mention, ad campaign, blog comments and any other types of mentions in the digital world.

Some terrific tools exist to simplify your online reputation management and significantly reduce the amount of time you spend doing so. The below mentioned tools are different – some free while others require a monthly fee.

Trackur

This social media tracking tool immediately alerts you when your brand is mentioned online. This is important because you can instantly respond appropriately, allowing you to respond timely even without scrolling through your Twitter feed all day. Trackur also has built in analytics that will advance your monitoring management by tracking trends and how to receive positive marketing responses. It does come at a monthly fee as well as a free basic plan.

Namyz

This wonderful tool actually lets you in on the details of your social influence. Social influence is deeply connected with online reputation. A special feature called RepScore rates your influence on different social media networks like LinkedIn, Facebook, Twitter, Google + and others. Other tools found in Namyz help grow your personal brand. It does this by tracking your visitors, and in comparing your success with that of your peers and leaders in that industry, all while monitoring search engines such as Google and Bing for social mentions. All of these helpful features to boost your brand performance are offered by Namyz on a single dashboard. They have a free basic plan, and monthly premium plans.

BrandsEye

BrandsEye has developed and combined many useful features which alert you through email whenever your brand is mentioned online. It also compares metrics with your internal data and monitors your conversations. The tool pinpoints where your brand has been mentioned in conversations. BrandsEye is one of the more expensive online tracking tools per month.

Rankur

This application allows you to discover new trending topics, monitor your social media presence more effectively while allowing you to track and manage your online reputation all at once. It's vast marketing capabilities enable you to tune and utilize its features in a way that best suits your needs and enhances your online presence. Rankur provides a free basic plan allowing you to determine if it will be effective for you. The apps paid options offer more features as part of a per month membership.

SocialMention

Social Mention is one of the few completely free tools. This social media tool searches the Internet for mentions of your brand and notifies you. It also scours competitors and offers the option to narrow down your search to certain blogs, videos, pictures, conversations and other phrases that you are looking up. There are no automatic updates so you need to check the application from time to time.

Google Alerts

Google is constantly expanding and offering new features. Its tracking application, Google Alerts, has been used for a while in effectively applying its metrics for online reputation management. You can first set up the search terms or phrases that you want, like targeted niche keywords or your company name. The next step is to specify what types of results you want to see and how frequently you'd like to receive them. Real-time alerts for effective reputation management are sent via email. Like many Google tools, Google Alerts is free to use.

With several options to choose from with varying tools and prices, you'll be sure to find one that suits your needs and your budget. Take a few for a test run and you'll surprise yourself by their effectiveness and the positive impact they will have in managing your online reputation.

Unleash the Power of LinkedIn

There are countless social media networks for you to choose from, each with their own set of benefits and drawbacks. Committing yourself to only one network limits your ability to reach countless audiences. LinkedIn is one social network that is a *must use* for professional brand management.

LinkedIn is much more than a job seeking platform – it's a medium through which to spread your business message in a professional atmosphere. The social network has a strong reputation that is favoured by search engines and ranks high in Google, lending it great authority. When individuals are debating whether or not to conduct business with another, chances are that they are checking LinkedIn.

The benefits of LinkedIn are endless. Being able to develop a content-rich profile on an authoritative site that doesn't charge for membership is like hitting the social media jackpot. LinkedIn is a way for both B2B and B2C companies to reach new prospects as well as connect specifically with their target audiences. The search filters allows a company to carefully target a desired demographic through professions and region, enabling them to directly engage with that audience.

In the Beginning

The page creation guideline created by LinkedIn says it all.
It informs its members on how to follow the rules to get their
Company Page started. These guidelines are the main reason
why this site's content is highly ranked.

Exactly how do you start the company page? Well, first and foremost
you need to have a personal LinkedIn account. The profile must
contain an actual real name (first and last name) and must also have
been completed with a profile strength from intermediate to an all-star
level, while maintaining several connections at the very least.

You must list the position title you hold in the company, and provide
a business email address.

After completing the above mentioned steps, you need to fill out
the required fields for your Company Page, which are:

- Your Company's Name

- A Company Description

- The Type of Company: Public, Educational, Self-Employed,
  Governmental Agency or Organization, Non Profit, Partnership

- The Size of the Company (number of employees):
  myself only (self-employed), 2-10, 11-50, 51-200, 201-500,
  501-1000, 1001-5000, 5001-10000, 10001 and over

- The Company's Industry (LinkedIn offers a large list
  to choose from)

- How your Company Operates – Operating Status

The information required above will create the backbone
of your Company Page, with optimized, informative content.

Next, comes the visuals, which are as important as the content. Many underestimate the importance of visuals in the creation of their company page, yet the visuals are key because they spread your brand's logo and online image. Here are some tips to keep in mind when updating your visuals on your LinkedIn Company Page:

- The images must be 646 x 220 pixels in JPEG, PNG or GIF file extensions. Make sure that your brand's images aren't larger than 2 MB.

- On your product/services section you can incorporate a maximum amount of three banner images and three links for each one. When adding more than one banner, LinkedIn will automatically create a rotating module with the banners.

- The "Standard Logo" feature of the brand has to be 100 x 60 pixels.

Ripe With Content

Optimizing your LinkedIn page is vital in developing your online presence. For starters, your company page must be filled with updated information about your company, its services and products, goals, and its competitive edge. Make it ripe with content.

The company page also has to be utilized in terms of images. Try to use your company logo and a relevant cover photo. This will feature your brand's message and potential clients will recognize it easier.

Always strive to use all 2,000 allotted characters to detail your brand in the Company Description section. Another section is Specialties, where you can and should add up to 20. A Services and Products tab

can also be incorporated, where you can add more content
of what you offer and elaborate on specifics.

Research which keywords are being used when searching for
your services and incorporate them into your product or services
descriptions. In doing this, you will have a bit of a head start in
reaching and engaging with your targeted audience.

Fresh, ripe content is the most effective way to get noticed, so update
your Recent Updates section with some impressive company content.
To ease your schedule, connect your LinkedIn Company Page with
tools such as HootSuite that will allow you to schedule this content
ahead of time.

After completing all the required sections for your LinkedIn
Company Page, advertising is the last step. The most wonderful
aspect of LinkedIn ads is that they can be shown to targeted
audience. Targeting options include job position, geographic
location, company industry, skills, size and so on.

Before targeting your audience with hopes of engaging with them,
do your research. Figure out who your target audience is depending
on your advertising and demographic goals. Understanding this will
help you not waste your money and to spend it wisely. If your goal
is lead generation, then you can target individuals by their
professional titles.

Managing a profile on any social media platform takes time
and work, but LinkedIn is truly a platform that every professional
and business owner *must* be on.

Rules of Engagement

For most companies, the occasional negative comment is a small price to pay for the many benefits of connecting with customers online. When handled properly, it can turn into an opportunity to strengthen a damaged customer relationship and may even win you a fan for life.

–Diane Gottsman

Once you have people talking about your brand, you need to respond accordingly and be careful how you "read." When responding to your audience's questions through social media, you have to consider social media manners. It may sound complicated, but after reading these general rules, you'll feel more ease and confident in representing your brand's voice through your responses.

Social media inquiries or comments are similar to receiving a phone call in the office – you must learn how to properly and professionally communicate. It's extremely important to handle situations professionally, and say "we're sorry" when you must. Proper responses will nurture your relationships with customers and build stronger bonds. Remember that relationships build trust and trust builds loyalty. If you don't answer the phone, you might miss a potential client.

Negative reviews might also give you a chance to reflect upon your company and its policies. Some negative reviews are genuine and can be fixed if the customer complaints are taken care of.

There are many businesses that are too powerful (at least for now) and have a strong hold in their area. They don't care for many negative reviews and never try to improve their reputation. This can only work for so long for a business; the negligence will eventually backfire. Before that happens, analyze the problem and look for its solution. It will save you from an unnecessary negative online reputation or an even worse outcome.

In other cases, people will leave a bad review out of spite, and that's quite normal for businesses. However, what's key is to realize and understand how to manage a good reputation and not let a bad reputation build up. Some businesses have done it, and done it very well. Knowing how to handle a bad review will save your online reputation.

Your Online Presence Must be Your Top Priority

Building your online presence is necessary; your company's future depends on it. Always have a social media strategy to engage effectively and consistently with your audience. Use tools to monitor your social media accounts and schedule your updates when your audience would most likely read. Keep an eye open to see what people are posting about your brand, check out your comments from your Facebook page, Twitter, Instagram, blogs, but also review other sites which offer options to leave a review like Yelp, Trip Advisor and others.

Respond Fast

Social media can get pretty "unsocial" when you don't respond to comments. More so, if the ignored comment is negative, your neglect will spread like wildfire throughout the network. Check responses and engagement as fast as possible, because in a quick 30 seconds, thousands of people can see that comment.

Don't assume the stance "If I pretend it's not there, it'll go away"
because it will only make it worse.

In order to minimize the potential damage of a negative comment,
respond as quickly as possible. This will also help people see your
point of view, and support your decision as well after reading
your explanation.

Don't Delete Comments

Always know that when you delete a comment, it's as if you
are admitting to what is being said about you and are accepting the
guilt. No matter how much you dislike a critical comment, let it stay.
This way, you can reply to it, address it head on, and show that you
are aware of their dissatisfaction and are willing to take the extra
steps to offer them a solution.

The only reason you should delete a negative comment is if it contains
racist, offensive, or harmful content that can leave distaste amongst
your audience. If that is the case, then go ahead and delete it promptly.

When handling negative comments, the best thing you can do is to
ask to take the conversation offline. In general, this will not defend
you from the online attacks, but this is the best course of action to take
when you stumble into this type of situation. Take it one-on-one and
there will be no other parties commenting or replying. Simply try to
offer them a solution.

Have a read of this next Reputation Wrecking Ball for a clear case study
of *what not to do.*

A famous example of the biggest social media meltdown is at the expense of the Applebee's restaurant chain. A server posted an image of a receipt, criticizing the customer who left it, on the public forum Reddit.

The receipt said, "I give God 10% why do you get 18%?" (Stableford, 2013).

What was Applebee's course of action? The employee was fired by the famous brand because she violated customer policy. They posted a status on the company Facebook page stating that they wished this situation hadn't happened and that they have taken disciplinary procedures with a team member due to her violating a guest's right to privacy.

Their post accumulated more than 10K comments with customers remarking on the situation. Applebee's, wishing the attention would go away, began deleting comments, blocking people and continuously posting generic statuses and comments. This was a lesson for Applebee's, as well as for other companies, of how not to handle comments on social media.

It can also be really hurtful when your business is being criticized – the same business that you built with blood, sweat and tears. No matter how negative the comment or review may be, take a deep breath and do not let yourself get too emotional. When emotions get stirred, you will come off as aggressive rather than apologetic.

Always Apologize

You need to show that you care and that you're being proactive by apologizing publicly. These people (or person) had liked you on Facebook, and followed you on Twitter and Instagram. A bad experience made them less loyal to your brand, and they want you to listen to their story. It's your job to respond sincerely, quickly, and apologize to them publicly while offering them a solution.

An apology and solution should always go together, regardless of the nature of the complaint. Brands shouldn't overlook complaints through social media. Rather, they should consider them as important (if not more so) than a face-to-face complaint.

Are Bad Comments Multiplying?

It's normal to receive negative comments, but if you notice a pattern of continuous negative reviews and comments – it's probably your fault. This indicates that something may be wrong with your business and that you should seriously consider finding out what the problem is and how you can resolve it. Look at this as a positive experience. You may save your brand from something worse if you hadn't noticed the patterns.

Always address the problem head-on, in a timely manner, and offer the complainant an apology and a solution. In doing this, not only will you most-likely win over that client again, but you will be positively representing your brand and business and winning over future clients by your courteous and professional manner.

Attract and Engage

A social media strategy is a success
when you are able to engage and interact
with your target audience.

—John Rampton

Now that you're confident in how to steer your online reputation and fully understand the impact of social media, you're probably ready to dive in and start creating! You're ready to take your brand to the next level, right? Yes! Now, we must talk strategy. Don't make the mistake of bounding in blindly or you'll be sure to flounder.

You need to create a successful social media strategy that will consider your goals and objectives to truly engage with customers. Here are some elements that need to be considered for constructing a strategy that will build a successful social media presence from day one.

Consider Your Goals: Your goals are your long-term inspiration to which you're working toward. Identifying your goals will determine your path and inspire your decisions when developing your strategy. With goals in mind, focus will follow and your social media presence will be guided and purposeful.

Determine your set of goals. Identify at least three, all of which will be long-term and something to set your sights on. For most wishing to use social media for professional purposes, their goals are generally along the lines of creating brand awareness, connecting with potential and past clients or customers, and sculpting an appealing online reputation. Try and identify at least one personalized goal that is unique to your company. This will help guide your strategy to ensure that you stand apart from the competition.

Step 1: Get Smart

When long-term goals have been identified, we need a way to keep us on track in the present. To do this, we are going to create a list of objectives. Your objectives are a way by which you can measure your efforts and accomplishments. While your goals are broad and more ambiguous, objectives are straight-forward, to the point, and will guide you on your way to achieving those goals.

The most favoured approach in constructing effective objectives is using the SMART method. SMART objectives are S-specific, M-measurable, A-attainable, R-relevant, and T-timely. Let's take a quick look at these and run through constructing a common objective.

In this instance, we will start with a common goal of using social media as a way to generate leads. Here's how we turn this broad goal into a SMART objective:

Specific: Make your objective clear and avoid ambiguous terms. This is where we provide the WHO, WHAT, WHERE, HOW, and WHY details. Who are you targeting? What do you want to accomplish? Where are you going to generate these leads? How do you plan on reaching your market? Why is it important?

Measurable: Here is where we ensure that the progress of our objective is trackable. Rather than "Increase leads" we will identify by what percentage we want leads increased by or, better yet, the specific number of leads.

Attainable: Ambition is wonderful, but having an unrealistic objective sets you up for disappointment and failure. If you were able to generate 20 leads last month, would it be realistic to aim for 700 this month? Ensure that your objective is actually attainable.

Relevant: Consider if this objective is consistent with your other goals and objectives, and if it fits into your long-term plans. While it is commendable to have a long list of objectives, you are bound to lose sight of your goals if you focus on ones that will not meet those needs.

Timely: While your goals are long-term, your objectives are meant to establish a sense of urgency and prompt for immediate action. Always include a time limit in your objective.

Now that we know the elements of an effective objective, let's create one for lead generation. Here's an example: "Through social media efforts, generate 30 inbound leads per month by February 1st."

Step 2: Speak Their Language

Knowing the demographics of your audience is essential for many aspects of business, and your social media presence is no exception. You want to look for the best ways to reach your audience and know what content to post that will engage those groups. With a bit of research, you can identify which social media platforms your target audiences are using the most and discover the content that they are most engaged with.

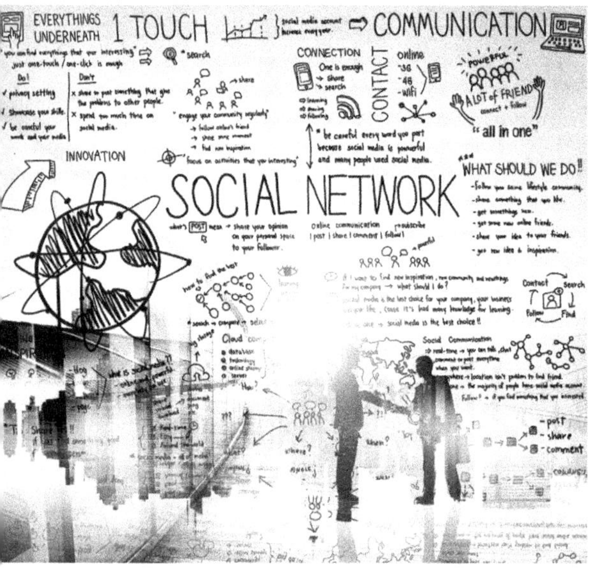

Here is your chance to dig a little. Create an average persona of an individual in your audience that includes his or her age, income, interests, habits, concerns, and professions. In learning about your desired base of clients, you will be equipped to appeal to them.

Many modern businesses are experimenting with seemingly unconventional channels in an effort to reach their audience and build business. To reach younger audiences, many are building connections on Instagram and Snapchat (Mears, 2015). In knowing who your audience is, you can better understand which social media platforms you should be devoting your time to.

Step 3: Social Listening

Remember that your goal is to reach your audience all while standing out from the competition. Researching your competition is crucial when you're planning to market your brand through social media.

You can research their tactics, consider incorporating some, but most importantly, gain insight into what they're *not* doing so that you can fill that gap. Keep in mind that what works for them may not work for you.

Put a list together of your main competitors (around four to five) and analyze what social media networks they use, how they interact with their audience and what type of content they are providing. When analyzing their content, take care to focus on their context, which can differ from humorous and light to formal and serious.

In terms of their engagement, you can actually measure it in order to receive a sense of how you stack up. For instance, review their latest 30 tweets on Twitter, and see how many favorites and retweets they have, which you can finally divide by the number of their total followers. The percent of follower engagement is vital in determining how effective their social media efforts are.

Of course, this isn't an accurate measurement, but it does offer insight to help you understand their engagement on social media. You can apply this simple formula on their other social media accounts.

Step 4: Narrow Down Your Options

After reading this far, you have a good understanding that there are too many platforms for one person to effectively manage. While it's normal to think that you need to create an account on every social media network that's popular, you may be wasting your time and energy. Your buyer persona is what you need to think about when choosing your channel. I have outlined the benefits and demographics of the most popular social media networks for you to refer to in the next chapter.

Step 5: Awesome Engaging Content

There's a beautiful connection between content and social media. Roughly said, without engaging content your social media is bland and meaningless. After you develop compelling content that would make your audience engage, the next step is to develop a content strategy.

A content strategy has a few components: the type of your content, what time you post, and the frequency at which you post it.

The type of content you post reflects your brand's voice in correlation with trends on the specific social media platform you're using. As to what time is best to post, you must experiment and find out. There are many research studies that claim certain times of the day as the best time to post – but that can only serve as an insight, not a rule. Your audience is unique and you need to test yourself to find out when they're the most active. There are various Web tools – TweetReach, Fanpage Karma, IconoSquare, etc – to track your peak engagement times. These tools will give you insight into the best times to post.

How often you post on various platforms is another important area to consider. The goal is to strike a fine balance between posting often enough that you are engaging, while not posting so often that you become 'spammy' and spark unfollows. The number of posts that are considered ideal vary depending on the platform, so do a bit of research and reference my guide in the next chapter.

Step 6: How Much and How Often?

Are you subscribed to social media monitoring tools? Are you incorporating email campaigns? Do you wish to advertise your company page on LinkedIn or Facebook? Like any marketing campaign, you need to plan your budget. Establish a budget that suits your strategy and is realistic. It's important that you have an overview of how much you're investing by developing an annual projection plan. Financially investing in building your online brand has the additional bonus of added incentive in keeping you accountable for managing and maintaining it.

Step 7: Avoiding Overlapping

When managing social media accounts with more than one person involved, it's advisable that roles are assigned to increase productivity and save from eventual "overlapping." It can be hectic and confusing at the start, but soon each team member will get used to their role as well as their tasks and obligations.

After the specific roles have been assigned, it's time to plan the execution. You and your team can develop daily or weekly plans on specific tasks regarding each specific role. Avoid monthly plans because they can get messy, become hard to manage, and new ideas may come along in a few days; therefore, it's better to stick with a tighter time-framed plan.

Useful tools exist to help you manage your team and have a more consistent and organized work-flow, saving you time and energy.

Every person's strategy will look different, but it is a crucial road map to help you navigate this new world. Draw a map that will ensure you arrive at your destination in a timely matter with the fewest possible accidents along the way.

Your Guide to the Top

In this day and age, with people changing the way they view and use social media, there really is no such thing as a 'one size fits all" platform. In fact, some businesses shouldn't be on certain social media platforms at all.

–Jason Falls

Facebook

With close to 1.4 billion users, Facebook is the heavyweight champion of social media. This social media platform has the widest appeal with the ratio of male to female users almost even. The ages of Facebook users are fairly balanced with 23.3% of users between the ages of 18-24, 24.4% of users between the ages of 25-34, and 31.1% of users falling in the age range of 35-52 (Paterson, 2015).

Nearly half of all the Internet users are on Facebook. Consequently, this is not a social media platform that you want to miss out on. Facebook is where everyone is! Fast Company suggests limiting posts to no more than two per day to avoid spamming your followers. For the best reach and engagement, schedule these posts to go live at 1:00pm and 3:00pm when the most users are active (Zephoria, 2015). With a cap of only two posts per day, be sure to make your content count. Here are a few posting ideas:

- The number of direct uploads of user videos per day exceeds those of YouTube so be sure to post any videos you create to your Facebook Page.

- Facebook is a great place to share the link to a new blog post, driving traffic to your website.

- Share engaging photos to add interest to your content. Captions on these photos should be between 100-250 words.

- Facebook is one of the best platforms to start a conversation with your clients. Ask your clients questions and opinions – "What do you think about the new barn door trend?" – to engage with them and create relationships.

LinkedIn

Often described as the Facebook for the professional world, LinkedIn is a social media website with a focus on networking. The platform has one of the highest membership numbers at 364 million users, "up from 296 million" (Statista, 2015a).

According to Guimarães, "Thirty-eight percent of college-educated adult Web users are on LinkedIn, compared to only 16% of those with some college education" (Guimarães, 2015). Guimarães also notes that the social networking site attracts 30 to 49 year olds more so than people of other age groups. "LinkedIn is also the only top social network to feature higher penetration rates in the 50-to-64 age bracket than in the 18-to-29 age group" (Guimarães, 2015).

A vibrant network of professionals, posting rules for LinkedIn are slightly different than those of Facebook. According to Fast Company, posting on the site once per day at 8:14 a.m. is optimal.

As one of the oldest social networking sites, having been created in 2002, LinkedIn has proven that it's here to stay and is an important way to attract new clients. Here are a few ideas to get you started:

- Always keep in mind that LinkedIn is a professional network so ensure that you're posting content that is industry-focused.

- Save your best content for early in the week when engagement rates are at their highest.

- Self-improvement topics such as success, productivity, and leadership have the most shares and views.

Twitter

Twitter is the social networking site that allows you to share frequent snippets rather than involved posts. There are 284 million active Twitter users that frequent the site with slightly more male engagement as they make up 56% of the network's users. Twitter is definitely most popular among the younger generation with 35% of the site's members falling in the age range of 18-29, and 20% sitting between 30-49 years of age (Jetscram, 2014). Used by 23% of entire adult population, the social media site is more popular among people under 50 (Pew Research Center, 2015).

This microblogging site allows users to express themselves in 140 characters or less. While Twitter might limit the number of characters per post, you are much less limited when it comes to posting etiquette on this platform. Unlike most social networks which have ideal posting frequencies of only a few times per day, Twitter users like to see accounts that post multiple times per day. Fast Company says that, for most followers, the ideal Twitter account will post 14 times per day and never more than once per hour (Lee, 2014).

Experts suggest that for an international reach you should schedule posts starting at 3:00am, but to reach local audiences, scheduling a post every hour between 7:00am and 11:00 pm is ideal.

According to Internet Live Stats, there are more than 500 million tweets sent each and every day. Here are some tips to ensure that yours stand out:

- Don't waste your 140 characters on lengthy links. Create a Bitly URL to shorten the link and include that in your tweet, using your remaining characters to catch the attention of your followers.

- Hashtags and keywords are important to extend your reach on Twitter. Carefully research your hashtags and create a list of your go-tos that are most effective.

- Look at the trending topics and create content that tastefully and effectively relates to them.

- Upload photos and short videos directly to Twitter, rather than sharing on Twitter via another network. This will allow your media to show up directly on your profile and be automatically visible in your followers' feeds.

- Check out the Twitter profiles of your competitors and see what they're posting that garners engagement (likes and retweets). Be sure not to copy them, but it will give you an idea of what works for your target market (Internetlivestats.com, 2015).

Instagram

Instagram is a photo-focused social network that has experienced one of the fastest levels of growth in users over the last couple of years. Instagram currently consists of a much younger audience with a whopping 53% of Internet users aged 18-29 belonging to the network.

This age group makes up 37% of Instagram's user base with just 18% of its users falling in the 30-49 years range (Pew Research Center, 2015).

While typical Instagram users are younger than the above networks, 57% of those users access the site or app daily. That's 150 million sets of eyes ready to see your content! Instagram etiquette suggests limiting yourself to three posts spread out throughout the day. To make them count, time your photos so that they're posted between the hours of 9:00 a.m. and 6:00 p.m. for optimal engagement (Jetscram, 2014).

This visual social network is quickly gaining popularity and is one of the most effective networks to reach younger audiences. Here are a few tips that will make your Instagram profile unforgettable:

- Instagram is all about beautiful and interesting images, so be sure that every photo you upload is high quality and visually appealing. You don't need to be a professional photographer or have an expensive camera, just try and harness the power of natural light and a still hand.

- Your feed of images reads as one large grid of photos, so try and tell a story or find a theme. You may choose to post only black and white photos or have a feed that's solely vibrant color. Stand out from the crowd by discovering your unique style.

- Instagram users love interesting backgrounds. When taking photos of objects, try an all white background for a professional crispness or mix it up by photographing it on fun fabric or against a brick wall.

- Even more so than Twitter, hashtags are how users stumble across your images. Find your list of ideal hashtags and save them to quickly copy and paste onto each image. To avoid looking spammy, don't include hashtags in the actual caption of the photo, but add them to a comment on your photo after publishing.

- Lastly, Instagram consists of many tight-knit communities that constantly interact. Find the niche you fit into (home decor, fashion, beauty, cars, home design), follow others in that community, and frequently like and comment on their photos.

Pinterest

Businesses often overlook Pinterest and all that it offers. While there are fewer users than Facebook, Twitter, LinkedIn, and Instagram, 70 million users log-in to the inspiration-board site. Although this number may not seem like a large enough audience to devote much time to the site, Pinterest's user-base is extremely targeted. Of those 70 million users, a whopping 88% of them have purchased a product that they've pinned (Petrovic, 2015). This shows us that Pinterest users turn to the site for buying decisions and are frequently inspired by the content they see.

Over 80% of Pinterest users are female, with 27% of them between the ages of 18 and 29, and 24% of them falling in the range of 30-49 (Jetscram, 2014).

There are few rules when it comes to Pinterest posting etiquette. To hold the attention of an active follower base, it is suggested that you post or repin at *least* five pins per day, with optimal pinning time being around 3:00 p.m. Here's how to get the most return on time on Pinterest:

- Pinterest users love organization so be sure to spend time setting up your boards and carefully categorizing them. A real estate agent might categorize boards by style of homes, while being sure to include DIY's, home-improvement projects, and around-the-house tips to round-off their audience.

- If you're using Pinterest to draw audiences to blog posts, ensure that your images are high-quality and consider adding text to your pinned image to encourage click-through. For example, rather than simply pinning a photo of a home with a "sold" sign on the lawn, draw your followers in by adding text to the image that reads "Top 5 Things You Need For a Quick Sale".

- Comments and favourites have little importance on Pinterest – it's all about the re-pins!

Google+

This is one social networking site that offers far more for businesses and personal branding than it does for personal use. Content on Google+ ranks higher in search engines so it should be a key place for businesses to share important information such as contact, reviews, and promotions.

With 363 million users, Google+ is one of the titans of social media. Interestingly, of those users, 70% of them are male and 40% of which are single (Ganot, 2014).

Fast Company suggests that correct Google+ etiquette allows for two posts per day. Seek the highest engagement on these posts by scheduling them for 9:00 a.m. and 7:00 p.m. when users are most active (Lee, 2014).

Here are a few tips that will help you see success from Google+:

- Keep both a business page and a personal profile. After you post content from your business page, use your personal profile and share it with your circles.

- As with Facebook, encourage engagement with links and posts on Google+ by asking users a question or for their opinion. Create that connection with your circles by engaging them in your content.

- Google+ is one of the rare social media networks in which your content can be formatted. Without going overboard, use bold, italics, and indentations for effect and to be attention-grabbing.

- On Google+, a high number of followers not only looks good but also boosts your authority on Google. Be sure to add those in your industry, professional acquaintances, and potential clients to your circles to encourage them to do the same.

- When asking for reviews from customers, consider adding a Google+ link for them to leave reviews directly on your profile. This will build credibility and set you apart from competitors.

- Google+ allows you to group connections into different circles so consider segmenting potential clients into separate circles. From here, you can strategically share posts with each target market.

YouTube

Almost everyone has heard of YouTube, the world's most popular video-sharing website. Since the website was purchased by Google in 2006, it has grown to over a billion users – almost 1/3rd of all people on the Internet. All of these users collectively create 4 billion video views per day (Smith, 2014). With numbers like these, you would think that businesses would capitalize on this waiting audience but just a fraction of small businesses use YouTube (Smith, 2014).

Here are a few ways in which your business can fill this gap on YouTube:

- Assert yourself as a professional in your field and create industry-specific how-to videos. A bakery may choose to create cake-decorating videos, while a real estate agent would consider uploading home-staging tips.

- Embed your YouTube videos into blog posts and post on other social networks to grow your subscribers and your audience.

- Carefully tag your videos so that they are searchable to users. Create a go-to list of tags that relate to the theme of your videos and brainstorm more that are similar. A pet store might create a YouTube channel with tips on caring for pets but will miss out on potential viewers if they only tag "dog" and "cat." To expand their reach, the pet store could get creative and add "pooch", "puppy", "hound", etc.

- As with many of the platforms in this guide, YouTube is a community. Engage with other content creators and other companies or organisations that you support.

- Remove any spam or particularly offensive comments as fast as possible. Again, do not automatically delete any negative comments, just like on any other platform. However, comments that are particularly offensive and unnecessary should be removed as soon as you see them.

Periscope

Periscope is a live-broadcasting app that was released in March 2015 after it was purchased by Twitter. The video app allows users to broadcast and watch videos live across the world. Once the broadcast is finished, it is saved for 24 hours for viewing by those who have missed it or wish to experience the excitement all over again.

While there is an app for Periscope, it's affiliation with Twitter
has enabled live feeds to be viewed right from the social media
platform's news feed.

As of August 10th, 2015, only four months following the app's release,
it hit 10 million active accounts and is currently the fastest growing
social media network to date (Medium, 2015). Every day, the app's
active users are viewing 40 years worth of content just on the
smartphone apps (Medium, 2015).

Because of the relative newness of Periscope, the majority
of brands and businesses have yet to embrace it which leaves
business owners with a huge, unsaturated market that *wants* more
content. The location-specific broadcasting feature makes it ideal
for reaching a geographically-segmented audience and the "behind
the scenes" nature of Periscope creates an entirely different
customer experience.

How can you use Periscope for your brand?

- Create interactive demos for a new product or service launch.
  Don't merely *tell* your customers how to use your product,
  but *show* them all while building a sense of community.

- Hold live group support on Periscope. Convey to your customers
  and clients that you care and want to answer their questions
  and troubleshoot any issues with full transparency.

- Periscope is the perfect place for brand announcements
  or to introduce a new line.

Snapchat

Snapchat is one of the newer social networks with a sole aim of
connecting individuals. Snapchat users take a photo or video, can add
any words, drawings, or emoticons to it, and then set the timer for it

to last between 1-10 seconds. From there, users can either message their photo directly to a Snapchat friend or upload it to their "story" which is like a media newsfeed. All images can only be viewed for the number of seconds set by the sender and story images disappear after 24 hours.

The audience of Snapchat is much younger than almost any other network with 45% of their user base falling in the age range of 18-24, and 26% of their users sitting in the 25-34 rage (Hoelzel, 2015).

This, coupled with the short live-time of its media, have resulted in most businesses not jumping on this social app. However, Snapchat has been very successful in engaging audiences and giving them a "behind the scenes" look into brands. Several brands that have been successful in doing this are: McDonald's, Audi, Taco Bell, and Mashable. This app is helpful in further driving that connection with your target audience and humanizing your brand.

In knowing your target audience, you will be able to locate within this guide which platforms they are using. Choose the ones that are most effective in reaching your readers and engage on those platforms regularly. Do keep up to date with other useful apps coming on the scene too, such as Slack, a wildly popular collaboration tool that is tipped to eventually replace workplace emails. Social media is constantly evolving, constantly changing and there is always more to learn.

Avoid Extinction

> *It is not the strongest of the species*
> *that survive, nor the most intelligent ones,*
> *it is those that are most responsive to change.*
>
> —Charles Darwin

The global reach of the digital age allows us endless possibilities. Furthermore, the promise of success is near-limitless. Because of this, the message we send online is even more powerful at times than the message we reveal in person.

We live in exciting times of both danger and opportunity. Many businesses and individuals have adapted to the rapid changes in new technology and utilized the phenomenal power and reach of the Internet for their own good. Therefore, the key to successfully navigating the online world is mindful management and the ability to adapt to changing conditions.

There are countless success stories linked to social media. From artists who got their big break on YouTube, startup businesses that skyrocketed to multimillion dollar revenue in a short time, or bloggers who create income in the six-figures, all types of people have benefited from social media.

However, keep in mind that some businesses have fallen away because they did not adapt quickly enough to stay relevant to their consumers in an online world.

Again, Brian Solis has provided cutting-edge research and insight in this area. He introduced the concept of Digital Darwinism and explained it as: "An era in which society, consumer behavior,

and technology are evolving faster than businesses' ability to keep up"
(Solis, 2011).

The business world is once again in a process of natural selection:
survival of the fittest. The winners will be those businesses and brands
who "get it," who position themselves to constantly adapt to change,
learn and understand about the digital landscape and provide their
customers the experience that they really want. Others face extinction.
Solis warns, "Digital Darwinism does not discriminate. Every business
is threatened."

What does this mean to you? In a nutshell: Don't let your business
become a dinosaur.

Best defence, good offence

In 2014, over 1,000 new apps were released daily (Statista, 2015b)
and an immeasurable number of new websites are created every day.
The rapid speed by which the online world changes may be daunting,
but it is critical that we keep up and are always looking ahead to
what is next. Looking to the future, it is only a matter of time before
individuals discover ways in which they may harness the weight
of this technology into a deliberate professional attack on others.

In fact, these premeditated attacks have already begun in lesser
forms by way of hate sites, though they may be rare. An app with
seemingly similar motives garnered global media attention when
it was announced to be released. This app, 'Peeple', was built on the
premise of rating *people* rather than places. It welcomed friends,
family, and acquaintances to create a profile for the people they knew
and rate their personality and character. Tagged as "Yelp for humans,"
anyone who had a Facebook page and your phone number was
welcomed to give you a rating "professionally, personally,
and romantically" (Statista, 2015b).

This app is a prime example of why we must be constantly
aware of new trends in social media that threaten our online
reputations. The best offence is a good defense and the best way
to fight (almost inevitable) online assaults is to be proactive in your
reputation management. A trusted presence online is sure to dilute
any negative onslaught.

Our online reputations have a real world value. They are the new
social currency. I recommend that you invest in yours, develop it,
nurture and protect it. By doing so, you will not be threatened by
this powerful new super-connected technological landscape. Instead,
you can embrace it, enjoy it, and leverage it to your best advantage.

If you carefully curate your content, practice transparency, and take
care of your brand, you will ensure that your reputation is safe online
and you look ethical, trustworthy, and respectful to potential
customers from the very first impression.

Bibliography

Adams, S. (2013, March 14). 6 Steps To Managing Your Online Reputation. *Forbes*. Retrieved from http://www.forbes.com/sites/ susanadams/2013/03/14/6-steps-to-managing-your-online-reputation

Agius, A. (2015, April 23) The 4 Essentials to Building Your Brand on Social Media. Retrieved From http://www.entrepreneur.com/article/244677

Anderson, M. (2014, July 7) 88% Of Consumers Trust Online Reviews As Much As Personal Recommendations. Retrieved From http:// searchengineland.com/88-consumers-trust-online-reviews-much-personal-recommendations-195803

Belicove, M. (2012, March 14). A New Study Reveals the Power of First Impressions Online. Retrieved from http://www.entrepreneur.com/article/223150

Bostrom, N. (2007). Speech presented at the Institute for Ethics and Emerging Technologies. Retrieved from http://izquotes.com/quote/212547

Botsman, R. (2010, May). Rachel Botsman: The case for collaborative consumption | TED Talk | TED.com [Video file].

Butzbach, A. (2014, Aug 14). 62 percent of Millenials research products on Facebook before buying. Retrieved from http://www.brafton.com/news/62-percent-millennials-research-products-facebook-buying/

Buzzfeed. (2013, May 22). 19 Companies that Made Huge Social Media Fails. Retrieved from http://www.buzzfeed.com/ariellecalderon/19-companies-that-made-huge-social-media-fails#.jlV1b1y24

Charlton, G. (2015, July 8). Ecommerce consumer reviews: why you need them and how to use them. Retrieved from https://econsultancy.com/ blog/9366-ecommerce-consumer-reviews-why-you-need-them-and-how-to-use-them/

Citroen, L. (2014, Jan 21). The ABCs of Personal Branding. Retrieved from http://www.socialmediatoday.com/content/abcs-personal-branding

Conner, C. (2014, March 4). Top Online Reputation Management Tips for Brand Marketers. *Forbes*. Retrieved from http://www.forbes.com/sites/ cherylsnappconner/2014/03/04/top-online-reputation-management-tips-for-brand-marketers/

Cruz, L. (2011, April 5). "Socialnomics": When Word of Mouth Goes Global. Retrieved from http://newsroom.cisco.com/feature-content?type=webconte nt&articleId=5994144

Debaise, C. (2013, July 29). The Art of the Response on Social Media. *Entrepreneur*. http://www.entrepreneur.com/article/227580

DeMers, J. (2014, November 3). How One Hotel Ruined Its Reputation By Penalizing Negative Reviews. Retrieved October 26, 2015, from http://www.forbes.com/sites/jaysondemers/2014/11/03/how-one-hotel-ruined-its-reputation-by-penalizing-negative-reviews/

DeMers, J. (2015, May 28). The Top 10 Benefits of Blogging On Your Website. *Forbes*. Retrieved from http://www.forbes.com/sites/ jaysondemers/2015/05/28/the-top-10-benefits-of-blogging-on-your-website

Dental Design (2015, Aug 15). Google+ Begins Rolling Out Vanity URLs. Retrieved from https://dental-design-products.co.uk/google-begins-rolling-out-vanity-urls

Dialog Marketing (2012). Reputation Management and Good Online Reviews. Retrieved from http://www.dialogmarketingservices.net/reputation-management-and-good-online-reviews

Digby, J. (2010, Oct 26). 50 Facts about Customer Experience. Retrieved from http://returnonbehavior.com/2010/10/50-facts-about-customer-experience-for-2011

Ganot, R. (2014, Nov 27). Google+ Demographics for 2014 and 2015. Retrieved from http://www.codefuel.com/blog/google-demographics-for-2014-and-2015

Georgia Local Marketing, 2014 http://www.georgialocalmarketing.com/ seo-athens-ga

Giacobbe, A. (2014, May 21). 6 Ways Social media Can Ruin Your Life. Retrieved from https://www.bostonglobe.com/magazine/2014/05/21/ ways-social-media-can-ruin-your-life/St8vHIdqCLk7eRsvME3k5K/story.html

Griwert, K. (2012, Feb 2). 89 percent of consumers use search engines for purchase decisions. Retrieved from http://www.brafton.com/news/89-percent-of-consumers-use-search-engines-for-purchase-decisions

Guimarães, T. (2015, Feb 27). The demographics that make LinkedIn's audience so valuable to businesses. Retrieved from businessinsider.com/ linkedin-as-a-marketing-and-brand-platform-2014-9?r=US&IR=T

Helm, B. (2014). Airbnb Is Inc.'s 2014 Company of the Year. Inc. Retrieved from http://www.inc.com/magazine/201412/burt-helm/airbnb-company-of-the-year-2014.html

Help Scout (n.d.) 75 Customer Service Facts, Quotes & Statistics. Retrieved from http://www.helpscout.net/75-customer-service-facts-quotes-statistics

Hepburn, A. (2011, Jan 18). Facebook Statistics, Stats & Facts for 2011. Retrieved from http://www.digitalbuzzblog.com/facebook-statistics-stats-facts-2011

Hoelzel, M. (2015, June 29). UPDATE: A breakdown of the demographics for each of the different social networks. Retrieved from http://www.businessinsider.com/update-a-breakdown-of-the-demographics-for-each-of-the-different-social-networks-2015-6

Houssem, D. (2014, July 16). 8 Essential Elements of a Social Media Strategy. *Social Media Examiner*. Retrieved from http://www.socialmediaexaminer.com/essential-elements-social-media-marketing-strategy/

HubSpot (2015). The Ultimate List of Marketing Statistics. Retrieved from http://www.hubspot.com/marketing-statistics

Internet live stats (2015). Twitter Usage Statistics. Retrieved from http://www.internetlivestats.com/twitter-statistics/

Ipsos. (2012) Interconnected World: Shopping and Personal Finance. Retrieved from https://www.ipsos-na.com/download/pr.aspx?id=11513

Isaacson, K. and Peacey, S. (2012). Human Resources and Social Media. *KPMG*. Retrieved from https://www.kpmg.com/US/en/IssuesAndInsights/ArticlesPublications/Documents/human-resources-social-media.pdf

Jetscram. (2014, Oct 20). Social media User Statistics & Age Demographics for 2014. Retrieved From http://jetscram.com/blog/industry-news/social-media-user-statistics-and-age-demographics-2014/

Kasper, K. (2012, July 9). Jobvite Social Recruiting Survey Finds Over 90% of Employers Will Use Social Recruiting in 2012. Retrieved from http://www.jobvite.com/press-releases/2012/jobvite-social-recruiting-survey-finds-90-employers-will-use-social-recruiting-2012

Kemp, S. (2015, Jan 21). Digital Social & Mobile Worldwide in 2015. Retrieved from http://wearesocial.net/blog/2015/01/digital-social-mobile-worldwide-2015

Knowem (n.d.). About Knowem, LLC. Retrieved July 17, 2015 from http://knowem.com/about-us.php

Kumar, S. (2009, July 9). Singer's revenge on United: A hit song. Retrieved from http://themoneytimes.com/20090709/singers-revenge-united-hit-song-id-1075860.html

Laudig, M. (2010, Aug 2). Ouch! Today's Hard Lesson on Yelp. *Phoenix New Times*. Retrieved from http://www.phoenixnewtimes.com/restaurants/ouch-todays-hard-lesson-on-yelp-6534055

Lee, K. (2014, April 15). The Social Media Frequency Guide: How Often to Post to Facebook, Twitter, LinkedIn, and More. Retrieved from http://www.fastcompany.com/3029019/work-smart/the-social-media-frequency-guide-how-often-to-post-to-facebook-twitter-linkedin-a

Leonard, I. (2015, May 9). Mistaken Mum Shames 'creep Photographing Her Children' When He Was Actually Taking Star Wars Selfie. *Mirror*. Retrieved from http://www.mirror.co.uk/news/world-news/mistaken-mum-shames-creep-photographing-5661707

Lickerman, A. (2010, April 22). The Value of a Good Reputation. *Psychology Today*. Retrieved from https://www.psychologytoday.com/blog/happiness-in-world/201004/the-value-good-reputation

Matsuo, Alex. (2014, July 16). 6 Of The Worst Lies Caught On Social Media. Retrieved from http://www.therichest.com/rich-list/the-biggest/6-of-the-worst-lies-caught-on-social-media

McCarthy, C. (2010, March 19). Nestlé mess shows sticky side of Facebook pages. Retrieved from http://www.cnet.com/news/nestle-mess-shows-sticky-side-of-facebook-pages/

McKeon, M. (2010). The Evolution of Privacy on Facebook. Retrieved October 20, 2015, from http://mattmckeon.com/facebook-privacy/

Mears, T. (2015, Oct 1). You Might Find Your Next Real Estate Agent on Instagram or Snapchat. *USNews*. Retrieved from http://money.usnews.com/money/personal-finance/articles/2015/10/01/why-real-estate-agents-and-homebuyers-should-use-instagram-and-snapchat

Medium. (2015, Aug 12). Periscope, by the numbers. Retrieved from https://medium.com/@periscope/periscope-by-the-numbers-6b23dc6a1704

Miguel, R. (2012, April 30). Social Media and Customer Service: An Update On "United Breaks Guitars" and Dave Carroll. Retrieved from http://splashmedia.com/archive/social-media-and-customer-service-united-breaks-guitars

Mooney, A. (2007). *Pressing the right buttons: People skills for business success*. Auckland, N.Z.: Random House New Zealand.

Namechk. (n.d.) Namechk | Username & Domain Search. Retrieved July 17, 2015 from https://namechk.com

Neate, Rupert. (2015, Aug, 17). Once-sexy American Apparel looks impotent in face of impending doom. *The Guardian*. Retrieved from http://www. theguardian.com/business/2015/aug/21/once-sexy-american-apparel-looks-impotent-impending-doom.

New Zealand Press Association (2006, March 8). Trade Me sold for $700m. *The New Zealand Herald*. Retrieved from http://www.nzherald.co.nz/ business/news/article.cfm?c_id=3&objectid=10371268

Noronha, C. (2015, Aug 21). Ashley Madison faces $578M Canadian class-action lawsuit. *Star Advertiser*. Retrieved from http://www.staradvertiser. com/news/breaking/20150821_Ashley_Madison_faces_578M_Canadian_ classaction_lawsuit.html?id=322574471

O'Hara, C. (2013, November 20). 10 Things You Need To Know About Online Reputation Management. Forbes. Retrieved from http://www.forbes.com/ sites/learnvest/2013/11/20/10-things-you-need-to-know-about-online-reputation-management

Paterson, M. (2015, May 4). Social media Demographics to Inform a Better Segmentation Strategy. Retrieved from http://sproutsocial.com/insights/ new-social-media-demographics/#facebook

Petrovic, Y. (2015). 10 Amazing Facts About Pinterest Marketing That Will Surprise You. Retrieved from http://www.jeffbullas.com/2015/02/26/10-amazing-facts-about-pinterest-marketing-that-will-surprise-you

Pew Research Center. (2014). Social Networking Fact Sheet. Retrieved from http://www.pewinternet.org/fact-sheets/social-networking-fact-sheet

Pew Research Center. (2015). Demographics of Key Social Networking Platforms. Retrieved from http://www.pewinternet.org/2015/01/09/ demographics-of-key-social-networking-platforms-2

Popkin, H. (2009, March 27). Getting the skinny on Twitter's 'Cisco Fatty'. *NBC News*. Retrieved from http://www.nbcnews.com/id/29901380/ns/ technology_and_science-tech_and_gadgets/t/getting-skinny-twitters-cisco-fatty

Schauer, P. (2015, Sept 27). Why Yik Yak Poses a Threat to College Campuses. *Social Media Today*. Retrieved from http://www.socialmediatoday.com/ social-networks/peteschauer/2015-09-27/why-yik-yak-poses-threat-college-campuses

Schumacher, S. (2015, Sept 15). Local SEO 101: Search Engine Optimization for Local Businesses. Retrieved from http://blog.surepayroll.com/local-seo-101-search-engine-optimization-for-local-businesses/

Short, K. (2014, Sept 9). DiGiorno Interrupts Serious Conversation About Domestic Violence To Sell Pizza. *Huffington Post*. Retrieved from http://www.huffingtonpost.com/2014/09/09/digiornos-pizza-whyistayed-tweet_n_5790504.html

Smith, C. (2014, April 21). By the Numbers: 120+ Amazing YouTube Statistics. Retrieved from http://expandedramblings.com/index.php/youtube-statistics

Social Mention (n.d.) About socialmention. Retrieved from http://socialmention.com/about

Solis, B. (2011). *The End of Business As Usual: Rewire the Way You Work to Succeed in the Consumer Revolution*. New York: Wiley.

Stableford, D. (2013, Jan 31). Applebee's fires waitress who posted receipt from pastor complaining about auto-tip. *Yahoo!*. Retrieved from http://news.yahoo.com/blogs/sideshow/applebees-waitress-fired-pastor-receipt-193820748.html

Statista (2015a). Numbers of LinkedIn members from 1st quarter 2009 to 2nd quarter 2015 (in millions). Retrieved from http://www.statista.com/statistics/274050/quarterly-numbers-of-linkedin-members/

Statista (2015b). Number of newly developed applications/games submitted for release to the iTunes App Store from 2012 to 2014. Retrieved from http://www.statista.com/statistics/258160/number-of-new-apps-submitted-to-the-itunes-store-per-month/

Stucker, M. (2014, March 4). Girl costs father $80,000 with 'SUCK IT' Facebook post. *CNN*. Retrieved from http://edition.cnn.com/2014/03/02/us/facebook-post-costs-father

TemboSocial (2014). Case Study: How Pfitzer Uses TemboSocial to Engage Employees. Retrieved from http://www.tembosocial.com/download-our-case-study-how-pfizer-uses-tembosocial-to-engage-employees

Trade Me (n.d.) Our story. Retrieved from http://www.trademe.co.nz/about-trade-me/our-story

Trimpe, A. (2011, February 21). The World Is Obsessed With Facebook [Video File] Retrieved from https://www.youtube.com/watch?t=44&v=xJXOavGwAW8

Tsarkov, E. (2013). Engaged Social Followers Are Your Best Customers. Retrieved from http://www.slideshare.net/etsarkov/engaged-social-followers-are-your-best-customers?qid=05e661d1-7cd0-4d31-93fd-a1ea3ff8eec0&v=qf1&b=&from_search=1

Tuerk, A. (2011, June 15). Me, Myself and I: Helping to manage your identity on the web. Retrieved from http://googlepublicpolicy.blogspot.co.uk/2011/06/me-myself-and-i-helping-to-manage-your.html

Valant, S. (2013, May 2013). Infographic: A Day In The Life Of The Internet. Retrieved from http://www.hostgator.com/blog/2013/05/02/a-day-in-the-life-of-the-internet

Zarrella, D. (2009). *The Social Media Marketing Book*. California: O'Reilly Media.

Zephoria. (2015, Oct). The Top 20 Valuable Facebook Statistics – Updated October 2015. Retrieved from https://zephoria.com/top-15-valuable-facebook-statistics

About the Author

Sarah Pearce has been the recipient of many national and international awards over the past 12 years. Sought after by many organisations for her unique blend of knowledge in real estate, business development and digital reputation, Sarah is now engaged full-time as a professional speaker, social strategist and business performance coach. Her speaking challenges the business community on their commitment to being relevant, visible and safe where their consumers increasingly are: online. In addition to coaching CEO's, senior executives, top agents and their teams, Sarah assists her clients to develop a powerful online brand presence with specialised training in Social Media Marketing and Brand Reputation. In her first book, *Online Reputation: Your Most Valuable Asset in a Digital Age*, she empowers the business community to maintain the upper hand in social media and protect their reputation in a constantly changing digital world.

Book Sarah Pearce as a speaker for your business or event

As a professional speaker, Sarah Pearce is sought after by many organisations for her unique blend of knowledge in real estate, business development and digital reputation. She brings a fresh perspective to the issues of trust and reputation in a changing world. "Social media is not a fad." Sarah warns, "It is a fundamental shift in the way we communicate, connect and experience life. It is also the language of our future consumers. Sarah challenges the business community on their commitment to being relevant, visible and connected where consumers now are: online. She delivers a punchy and captivating presentation in a language that everyone can understand.

"Sarah was a presenter at our annual regional (Asia, Pacific, Middle East, Africa) conference this year and the feedback from her session was outstanding. She delivered the information we needed in a way that was easy to understand and with great takeaways."
–Wayne Howett, CEO,
Ronald McDonald House Charities NZ

Read more testimonials
at **sarahpearce.co.nz**

To book Sarah for large and small groups as speaker, trainer, panelist or MC go to **sarahpearce.co.nz**

Notes

Notes

Notes

www.ingramcontent.com/pod-product-compliance
Lightning Source LLC
Chambersburg PA
CBHW060930050726
47592CB00003B/896